Guide to

CONSERVATION FOR METAL DETECTORISTS

RICHARD HOBBS,
CELIA HONEYCOMBE
& SARAH WATKINS

ILLUSTRATIONS BY KATE MORTON

TEMPUS

First published 2002

PUBLISHED IN THE UNITED KINGDOM BY:
Tempus Publishing Ltd
The Mill, Brimscombe Port
Stroud, Gloucestershire GL5 2QG
www.tempus-publishing.com

PUBLISHED IN THE UNITED STATES OF AMERICA BY:
Tempus Publishing Inc.
2A Cumberland Street
Charleston, SC 29401
www.tempuspublishing.com

British Library Cataloguing in Publication Data.
A catalogue record for this book is available from the British Library.

ISBN 0 7524 2376 2

Typesetting and origination by Tempus Publishing.
PRINTED AND BOUND IN GREAT BRITAIN.

Contents

List of illustrations   4

Acknowledgements   6

Foreword   7

PART I: BACKGROUND   9

  1   What is conservation?   9

  2   Metals used in the past   12

  3   Corrosion and 'original surfaces'   20

PART II: PRACTICAL ADVICE   27

  4   In the field   27

  5   At home: first steps, storage and signs of trouble   36

  6   Examining and recording finds   51

  7   Cleaning objects: professional approaches   57

  8   Popular cleaning methods to avoid   65

  9   Stabilisation treatments, coatings and lacquers   71

 10   Repair, reconstruction and restoration   75

 11   Displaying objects   79

PART III: APPENDICES   82

Appendix 1   Metal detecting in England and Wales   82

Appendix 2   Taking a map reference   86

Appendix 3   Contacts and suppliers   87

Appendix 4   Further reading   92

Index   93

List of illustrations

Text figures

1   Undisturbed archaeology and the effects of deep ploughing
2   Good practice: small holes should be made in polythene finds bags before a detecting trip
3   Good practice: taking a GPS reading in the field
4   Good practice: storing objects in the field
5   Bad practice in the field: the finder is rubbing his find on his sleeve, not recommended, and has not bothered to fill in holes from previous discoveries
6   Bad practice: washing finds in the nearest river is not recommended
7   Bad practice: washing finds under the tap is not recommended for the vast majority of finds
8   Good practice: working on finds in the home
9   Bad practice: fan heaters should not be used to dry finds
10 Good practice: storing objects in the home
11 Bad practice: harmful substances for metal finds

Tables

1   Melting and smelting temperatures for the metals of antiquity. *After Tylecote 1986*
2   Colour as a basic first clue to the identification of corroded metals
3   Suitable packing materials for objects
4   Storage environments for different materials
5   Spotting signs of trouble: indicators of active corrosion

Colour plates

1   Base silver snake ring from the Snettisham jeweller's hoard, Norfolk, before and after cleaning
2   Cross section of a copper-alloy dagger blade from the ancient Near East, showing the layered nature of the corrosion products
3   Cross section of iron tyre from Wetwang, East Yorkshire, dating to the Iron Age, with the shape of the object preserved in the corrosion products
4   The hilt of an iron sword with part of a well-preserved bone handle
5   Mineral preserved textile wrapping around an Iron Age copper-alloy torc from Snettisham, Norfolk
6   Mineral preserved textile on an iron object; textile fibres have been completely replaced by the iron corrosion products

7   Mineral preserved organic remains of wood and leather on the back of an Anglo-Saxon iron shield boss

8   Under magnification, the wood and leather remains of the iron shield (**colour plate 7**)

9   Excavation of a hoard of Iron Age metalwork in Hertfordshire

10 The hoard of Iron Age metalwork (**colour plate 9**) being lifted in a block

11 The hoard of Iron Age metalwork (**colour plate 10**) after excavation in the laboratory by a professional conservator

12 Good practice: storage materials for objects

13 Good practice: recently excavated finds packed in labelled polythene bags with additional 'Plastazote' foam for support

14 Signs of trouble. A close up of an iron object shows spots of orange liquid known as 'weeping'

15 Signs of trouble. Bright orange powdery areas of active corrosion are visible on this iron object

16 Signs of trouble. This lead token is very unstable, some parts of the edge have broken off and the visible white powder is active corrosion

17 Signs of trouble. Roman bracelet and bow brooch in poor condition

18 Signs of trouble. Here active spots of 'bronze disease' are clearly visible on the surface of a copper-alloy object

19 Anglo-Saxon corroded iron buckle and plate from Buckland cemetery, Kent, as discovered

20 X-radiograph of the iron buckle (**colour plate 19**)

21 The original surface of the iron buckle (**colour plate 20**) has been revealed by careful manual cleaning guided by the x-radiograph

22 Three-quarters-cleaned Anglo-Saxon silver-gilt brooch with garnet inlay

23 A conservator examining an Anglo-Saxon iron shield boss under a microscope with the help of an x-radiograph

24 A range of small hand tools used by a conservator

25 A silver coin which has been half-cleaned with a glass bristle brush. Scratches can be seen on the surface where the cleaning has been too harsh

26 A conservator using a pneumatic pen and a microscope to reveal the original surface of a copper alloy object

27 Fragment of a Roman copper alloy object, half-cleaned with a cotton wool swab dampened with industrial methylated spirits (IMS)

28 Bad practice: treatments to be avoided include table salt, denture cleaner and disinfectant

29 Bad practice: treatments to be avoided include denture cleaning fluid

30 Coatings and lacquers. This shows the protective properties and the potential damage of different wax coatings

31 A variety of good and stable display materials

32 Good and bad mounting methods for coins

Acknowledgements

A large number of people have helped in putting this guide together. Contributions to the text and editing were made by Adrian Tribe, Amanda Sutherland, Philip Macdonald and Siobhan Stevenson, and Kate Morton produced the line drawings. Thanks also to Trevor Springett, The British Museum photographer for the Department of Conservation. We would also like to thank all those, both amateur enthusiasts and professionals, who have commented on the various drafts: Bob Baldock, David Barwell, Simon Bean, Roger Bland, Margaret Brooks, Reg Bruce, Geoff Burr, Mike Corfield, Jeremy Davis, Vanessa Fell, Andrew Gardner, Alan Jackson, Ralph Jackson, Roy Lewis, Ian Medhurst, Stuart Needham, Norman Oxley, Ian Panter, M.N. Parker, Ceinwen Paynton, Claire Pinder, Ruth Scott, Colin Sharratt, Fleur Shearman, John Slade, James Stanfield, A.B. Steers, Kirsten Suenson-Taylor, Ciorstaidh Hayward Trevarthen, Bob Whalley, K. Wheatley and James Woodrow. The book was produced in consultation with the Archaeology Section of the United Kingdom Institute for Conservation. The authors would also like to acknowledge the support of the following organisations who allowed them time to complete this book: the Departments of Conservation and Prehistory and Early Europe at The British Museum, the Heritage Department at Cambridgeshire County Council, and the Portable Antiquities Scheme.

Foreword

One of the most common questions asked of all those involved in dealing with metal detector users is 'How do I clean my finds?'. Every year hundreds of thousands of metal artefacts are found by members of the public, the vast majority by the estimated 15,000 metal detector users thought to be regularly detecting on British soil. Finders are concerned about the long-term care and conservation of their objects, and this book offers some guidance on how these concerns might be met.

Before reading on, a number of very important points need to be made:

The primary aim of this guide is to inform finders of good conservation practice for their archaeological discoveries. There are no quick fixes or easy solutions when it comes to archaeological finds of any type. It is accepted that decisions on how to treat and care for individual artefacts ultimately rest with the owner. However, finders should remember that many artefacts are of historical or archaeological significance and will be of interest to a wide community of academics, researchers and the public in general. By treating finds correctly, and reporting them to the Portable Antiquities Scheme or local museum, finders can make an excellent contribution to understanding and looking after our heritage for the benefit of everyone.

Although this book is aimed principally at metal detectorists, it will also provide useful information to amateur fieldwalkers, other chance finders, and archaeologists working in both the voluntary and professional sectors. The focus of the work is on metal archaeological objects, as these are one of the most vulnerable categories of material; ceramics, worked stone, bone and other organic materials are beyond the scope of this work.

This book is also principally concerned with finds made on land as opposed to objects which have come from marine environments. For these types of find, reference should be made to Robinson 1998 (see Appendix 4).

The degree to which a find requires conservation and cleaning is dependent upon the object itself and its burial environment. When conserving an artefact, it is necessary to understand both its condition after excavation and the factors, such as burial environment, which have influenced this condition. This book explains how metal artefacts corrode and offers advice on their storage and packing to help minimise further deterioration. It also describes the types of treatments that might be carried out by a conservator in order to investigate a metal find through removal of dirt and corrosion.

This guide is NOT a manual on 'how to clean metal finds'. The fragile condition of these objects can be made worse by the application of quick and easy solutions. For this reason, we do not recommend that any untrained person carries out manual or chemical treatments on an archaeologically or historically important artefact. Instead we describe the inherent risks of any practical intervention so that owners have enough information to guide their decisions.

It is essential that any treatment is carried out using the correct health and safety precautions. The treatments carried out by professional conservators often involve substances that, if not properly used, can be dangerous to both artefacts and people. Many of the chemicals used are toxic or corrosive and may cause health problems if used incorrectly. Throughout this book we have attempted to identify health hazards associated with materials or corrosion products. No responsibility can be taken for omissions or for damage or loss arising from information contained in this book.

Finders are advised to seek the advice of a professional conservator. Sources of conservation advice are provided at the end of this book. Alternatively, finders can contact their regional finds liaison officer who will be able to point them in the right direction. A list of contacts is provided in Appendix 3.

An attempt has been made to keep scientific names to a minimum in this book. Where technical terms first occur in the text, every effort has been made to explain these, and they are also included in the index.

This book has been produced to assist the work of the Portable Antiquities Scheme, set up in 1997 to complement the Treasure Act. More information about Treasure and Finding our Past: the Portable Antiquities Scheme can be found in Appendix 1.

PART I: BACKGROUND

1 What is conservation?

Conservation is now a familiar and accepted term often used to describe the preservation of the natural environment – plants, animals and even landscapes. It is also used to mean the preservation of objects that are part of our cultural heritage. Archaeological conservation is concerned with objects that have been buried and retrieved (excavated) from the soil or water.

Conservation has two principal aims:

- to **preserve** the object;
- to **reveal** information.

The condition of a metal object removed from the ground is likely to be different from that of an object, made from the same material, that has never been buried. It may look different, it may be more fragile, and it may be susceptible to further deterioration. Its condition and appearance will depend on a wide range of factors including the type of material the object is made from, its condition when buried, and the nature of where it was buried.

When a buried object is removed from the soil, there is a sudden and drastic change to its environment. The change can so destabilise an object (which may have survived in the ground for hundreds of years) that its condition can deteriorate rapidly and irreversibly. The action taken to prevent such deterioration – usually by controlling the object's post-excavation environment (temperature, humidity, pollutants and light) – is known as preventive conservation.

Conservation can also involve physically treating objects using tools or sometimes chemicals: this is known as interventive conservation. This may involve examination and removal of corrosion, which may be needed to clarify the identification and form of an object. Such work can reveal evidence, surviving within the soil and corrosion layers, which indicates how the object was made or used. Other interventive methods include repair, like re-attaching a broken part, which may make an object more physically stable and more understandable. The same may be said for restoration, for example re-assembling broken pieces into the shape and form of the original complete vessel and filling missing areas.

Every object is different, and so the treatments devised by professional archaeological conservators are tailored to suit each individual object. In addition, there should always be a presumption in favour of preventive conservation. This means that objects are not treated by interventive means unless absolutely necessary.

When deciding on an appropriate degree of intervention and of preventive conservation for an object, a conservator needs to take account of:

- the nature and condition of the object;
- evidence that may be revealed and which also needs to be preserved;
- aesthetic considerations, i.e. how the object will look afterwards;
- the expectations of the user/owner;
- how the object will be used i.e. for display, for study, and so on;
- equipment and materials available;
- the skill, knowledge and expertise of the conservator who will do the work.

Conservators aim to keep the extent of interventive treatment to a minimum and to use reversible treatments where possible. The materials and chemical solutions used for conservation are tested by conservators and scientists to make sure they do not cause damage and that they can be removed and reversed at any time if necessary. Damage from inappropriate treatments may not be apparent immediately but may start to develop later. So that it is clear how an object has been treated, conservators keep records of all treatments as they are carried out.

Conservation is an evolving discipline. As examination techniques and available expertise improve, particularly in understanding evidence that may be preserved on or in association with objects, conservators are better able to understand the short and long term effects of treatments. It is now realised that some treatments undertaken in the past, with the best of intentions, would not be considered 'good practice' by today's conservators.

Who are conservators?

Conservators usually specialise in one field of conservation, such as paintings, textiles, books or archaeological objects. Within the field of archaeological conservation, conservators may specialise even further – wood, metals, ceramics or stone, and so on.

Conservators are skilled professionals, trained, often to university degree level and beyond, in the theory and specialised practice of materials conservation. They have detailed knowledge of materials science and the structure, chemistry and deterioration of materials from which objects are manufactured, as well as those that are used to conserve them.

Like many professionals, conservators are governed by codes of professional conduct that aim to maintain high standards of practice. The United Kingdom Institute for Conservation (UKIC) is the main professional organisation for conservators in the UK. Conservators who meet defined standards of practice may seek to be accredited under the Professional Accreditation of Conservator-Restorers Scheme (PACR) through UKIC (contact details are provided in Appendix 3).

Archaeological conservators play an important role in the archaeological process. They aid archaeologists and finds specialists in the recovery of information from excavated artefacts. Working with archaeologists, scientists and museum curators, they help to investigate, preserve and present evidence from the past.

Archaeological conservators can be found within public sector organisations, such as museums, archaeological units and universities. There are also some archaeological conservators who work independently. The Conservation Register (currently held by UKIC) is a database of conservation practices who undertake conservation commercially for the private sector. The Register is not a guarantee of competency but many practices may be staffed by accredited conservators.

In the next chapter, the range of metals which were used in the past will be examined in order to understand the types of material which may be discovered by metal detectorists and fieldwalkers.

2 Metals used in the past

Metals used in antiquity were gold, silver, copper, lead, tin and iron. (Modern metals such as aluminium were not used until recent times and are not discussed in this book). All these metals were used before official history begins in most of the British Isles, i.e. by the Roman period which began in AD 43. Metals were used on their own or mixed together (as alloys) to make objects.

Metals are rarely found in nature in their native, or metallic, form. The only metals that were available in antiquity in their native form were gold, copper and meteoric iron. Apart from gold, however, all the metals are more usually found mixed with other substances as minerals or ores. The ores have to be mined and then processed to extract the pure metal. The extraction of a metal from its ores requires heat and a reducing (no oxygen) atmosphere, in a process known as smelting. The technology needed to extract different metals from their ores took a long time to develop, with iron being the most difficult and therefore the most recent metal to be exploited. Even after processing, most of the metals used in antiquity were not really pure. They often still contained tiny traces of other substances. Identification of these impurities, or trace elements, can potentially be used to discover where the metals originally came from.

How metals were worked

Once extracted from their ores, all metals have a number of properties which enable them to be worked and made into objects. They have a crystalline structure. To a greater or lesser extent, depending on the metal, they are malleable; they can be made into an object by hammering (forging) or rolling, without breaking or cracking. However, metals can also become brittle, that is they can suddenly fracture or snap. The brittleness of a metal tends to increase if it is cold worked (by hammering or rolling) and also with age, as corrosion spreads at a microscopic level between the crystals. Brittleness can be reduced by heating the metal, a process known as annealing. Metals in decreasing order of malleability by hammering are gold, silver, copper, tin, lead, iron (wrought). Cast iron is not malleable. The order (decreasing) of malleability by rolling is different: lead being the most malleable followed by tin, gold, silver, copper.

Another property of metals is their ductility which allows them to be drawn into fine wire. However, malleable metals are not necessarily ductile; for example lead is very malleable but is not readily drawn into wire. The most ductile metal is gold, followed by silver, iron, and then copper.

All metals become liquid if heated to a high enough temperature – the melting point for that particular metal. In their liquid form, different metals can be mixed together to form alloys and also made into objects by casting, that is pouring the molten metal into a mould. Whether or not metals were made into objects by casting in antiquity depended upon the metalworkers having the technology to heat the metal to its melting point. An open campfire would not normally give a temperature higher than 700°C. The temperature of at least part of an open fire could be increased by inserting a pair of bellows. This could raise the temperature enough to smelt some copper and lead ores.

Table 1 gives the melting and minimum smelting temperatures for the metals used in antiquity. The actual smelting temperature needed to extract a pure metal from its ores varies with the composition of the ores, and could be considerably higher than the minimum possible.

Table 1   Melting and smelting temperatures for the metals of antiquity. *After Tylecote 1986*

Metal	Melting point °C	Minimum smelting temperature °C
Tin	232	600
Lead	327	800
Silver	960	800
Gold	1063	N/A
Copper	1083	400
Iron	1540	1100

The working history of a metal object – casting, cold working, annealing, and so on – is preserved in the crystal or grain structure; this metallographic structure is visible under a high power metallurgical microscope. Any conservation or restoration treatment that uses heat has the potential to destroy this metallurgical history of the object.

How metals were joined

Different parts of a metal object might be joined together by rivetting or by soldering. Soldering is when two parts of metal are joined together by a melted metal alloy, the solder, which flows between them. The solder is made of a metal alloy with a lower melting point than the metals being joined. The parts are joined by the solder diffusing into the base metal on either side of the join. Solders are generally described as being either hard or soft. Hard solders have higher melting points (*c.*600-700°C) whereas soft solders have lower melting points (*c.*300-400°C). Solders may be named either according to their main metal constituent, or by referring to the metal they are used to join. Soft solder is an alloy of lead and tin. Hard solders might be an alloy of gold with copper or copper and silver, or of silver alloyed with copper.

Another joining method, mostly used for iron, is welding – where the two pieces to be joined are heated to white heat. At this temperature, the iron is so soft and plastic that if two pieces touch and are then hammered, they will fuse together.

Gold

Gold occurs in its bright metallic, or native, state in nature. The earliest gold objects in Britain have been dated to about 2500/2400 BC, and these mainly comprise items of personal adornment, such as ear-rings.

The gold used in the past was seldom completely pure, either because of naturally occurring impurities such as silver, or because it was deliberately alloyed with silver or copper to improve hardness and strength and for economy (i.e. to make it go further).

The presence of impurities affects the colour of the gold. For example, a high silver content – at least 20 per cent in the natural alloy electrum – would give a white gold, whereas copper in the gold would give a much richer red/yellow colour. The surface colour and composition of a gold object may be different from that of the core metal due to the practice of increasing the gold content of the surface layer by a technique known as depletion gilding.

Gold is very malleable and ductile and therefore easily worked. It was most commonly used to make coins and items of jewellery, for example the Iron Age torcs in the famous Snettisham treasure from Norfolk. Gold objects were generally made by casting into a mould, as the finished object or as sheet metal which was then cold worked by beating and hammering into the shape of the object.

Gold was also used as surface decoration, for example by gilding. Gilding was used on a range of different materials including wood, ceramic and stone, as well as other metals. More elaborate decorative gold techniques include *filigree*, where differing lengths and thicknesses of gold wire were applied to the surface of the object; and granulation, a technique whereby small droplets of gold were applied to the surface as beads of different sizes.

Silver

The earliest silver artefacts in the British Isles are probably of Iron Age date (approximately 650 BC to 50 BC), although a simple bead is known which on stylistic grounds may date to the early Bronze Age (about 2500 BC) (Stuart Needham pers. comm.).

Sometimes pure metal was used, but extraction techniques to retrieve the metal from its ores often meant that even 'pure' silver contained impurities (often up to 5 per cent) of copper, lead and iron. It was also often deliberately alloyed with copper to produce base silver. The addition of copper tends to dull and discolour the metal (in very simple terms, the brighter the colour of the white metal, the purer the silver). In some Roman 'silver' coins, the copper content can be as high as 95 per cent, for instance the 'radiate' coin of the late third century AD. In these coins, a silver appearance would have been achieved by chemically removing the copper content from the surface creating a silver rich layer over a baser silver core.

In antiquity, silver was used to make a range of artefacts including coins, jewellery and vessels, and was applied to other metals as decoration. The most common silver finds are coins. Coins were made by casting and striking using dies. Before Roman times, silver finds are relatively rare. This is not necessarily because silver objects were not made; rather it may be a reflection of the fact that silver was so rare that it was repeatedly remelted and reused. Also silver corrodes rapidly in the ground if there is even a slight trace of salt present. In Roman times use of silver seems to have increased as Roman extraction of the metal from its ores became more efficient and large scale. Items of jewellery and silver tableware (for example, spoons) become more common in the archaeological record.

Silver vessels were made either by raising (hammering a flat cast disc, supported on a stake, into shape) or by casting into a mould. Casting seems to have become more common in the Roman period. Annealing would have been part of the raising process, to restore malleability to the metal, which would become increasingly brittle as it was hammered. Whether raised or cast, the surface of the object would then need further work to finish it. Raised vessels might be smoothed by planishing with a special hammer and then the surface might be polished with fine abrasive powders. Cast vessels might need to be finished on a lathe. Different parts of a vessel could be attached to one another by rivetting or by solder.

Different decorative techniques were applied to silver artefacts including gilding (gold) and inlay with black niello (silver sulphide). Not all silver in antiquity was intended to be bright shiny metal; sometimes the surface was coloured or patinated by deliberately corroding the surface of the metal to blacken it. Surface decoration might also be created by chasing (designs created using hammers and punches without removing any metal); engraving (design created with fine tools which remove some metal from the line) or embossing (also known as *repoussé*, when relief design is hammered out from the back using punches).

Silver was also used as a surface decoration (by plating or inlay) on other metals (copper alloys or iron). Sometimes an alloy of silver and tin was used rather than pure silver.

Copper and its alloys

The first use of copper to manufacture tools and weapons in the British Isles dates to approximately 2600 BC. Copper does occur in its native, or metallic, state in nature, although its surface would be covered with some corrosion, and the metal would not be so obvious as gold. Some of the earliest copper objects may have been made from native copper rather than from smelted copper.

In antiquity, copper was initially used on its own, but was later mixed with other metals to form alloys. Bronze, which is an alloy of copper with tin, was used in the British Isles from approximately 2400 BC. It is harder than pure copper and has a more yellow, rather than pinkish, colour. Lead was also sometimes added to bronze to improve its casting qualities. The amount of other metal mixed with copper affected the overall appearance and working properties of the alloy. For example, if the amount of tin added to the copper was more than 30%, the result was speculum. Speculum has a grey/white appearance and although brittle, would take a high polish, so it was used to make mirrors. Copper was also alloyed with zinc to make brass, but this was not exploited until the century prior to the Roman invasion of Britain, i.e. the first century BC. Without undertaking analysis, it is rarely possible to identify the alloy. Thus conservators and archaeologists tend to use the term 'copper alloy' rather than to speculate on the specific composition (e.g. bronze or brass).

Copper alloys were cast to form artefacts directly or into ingots from which sheet metal could be hammered out and then further shaped to form objects such as vessels. A wide range of artefacts were made from copper alloys, from tools and weapons to domestic items like buckets and cooking pots. It was also used to make items of jewellery and dress accessories, and coinage from the late Iron Age onwards. Objects ranged from the simple and functional (for example, a one piece brooch), to the very elaborate (such as a ceremonial shield).

When cast, copper alloys are relatively soft and malleable and can be shaped and hardened by hammering. The cutting edges of copper alloy tools were deliberately hardened in this way. However, as the metal is worked it becomes increasingly hard and brittle and will eventually crack and break unless its malleability is restored by heating (annealing).

Both rivets and solders were variously used to join parts of copper alloy artefacts in antiquity. Rivets or solder might be part of the original technology used when the object was made, or be evidence of an ancient repair.

Surfaces of copper alloy artefacts were sometimes decorated with other metals such as silver, tin and gold. Some copper alloys may appear to have a white/grey metal surface finish, which is not plating, but is the result of surface enrichment. This may have been done either deliberately, or was an accident of the casting process or was due to corrosion. Examination of the metal at a microscopic level is often needed to tell the difference. Deliberate patination of copper alloys also occurred in antiquity, in a similar manner to silver.

Lead and tin

Until relatively recently, the first use of lead in the British Isles was something of a matter of conjecture. However, in 1992, a grave was discovered in a cist cemetery in Peebleshire, Scotland, which appeared to provide the earliest evidence for the use of lead to make objects. The cemetery was dated to the Early Bronze Age (*c.*2100-1600 BC), and the lead artefacts consisted of 31 tiny beads found in one of the graves. (The full report of this find by Fraser Hunter was published in the journal *Antiquity* in 1994, volume 68, pages 824-30).

Lead was one of the easier metals to extract from its ore. The temperatures needed to smelt the main lead ore, galena (lead sulphide), could be easily reached in parts of a domestic fire or simple furnace. Major exploitation of the lead ores in Britain began with the Romans almost immediately after the invasion in AD 43. In the Roman period the molten lead produced by smelting was poured into rectangular clay moulds to form ingots, also called pigs. Lead pigs have been found with inscriptions dating them to AD 49. In this form lead was transported all over the Roman Empire, before being re-cast into objects. Lead sheet was made by casting molten lead into flat sand beds.

Lead ores were also important because they were the main source of silver in antiquity. After the lead had been extracted from the ore, a further process, known as cupellation, was used to extract the silver from the remaining slag and sometimes from the smelted lead itself. Cupellation required temperatures of about 1000°C to 1100°C.

In the Late Bronze Age, lead was used to make the patterns from which clay moulds for casting socketed axes were made. There have also been finds of impure lead and lead-tin solder in association with objects from this period. The majority of lead finds, however, are of Roman or later date, probably because lead in earlier periods was likely to have been reused. A major use for lead was for weights, such as loom-weights, or net-sinkers. Sheet lead was used for roofing and made into coffins, cisterns, and pipes. Lead is easy to work – it is soft and can be hammered and shaped at ordinary temperatures without becoming hard or brittle. Pipes, for example, were made by bending sheet lead around a wood former. The edges were sealed or welded together by pouring on molten metal. Decoration in sheet lead was usually cast in, the pattern having been imprinted in the sand bed on which the sheet was cast.

Lead artefacts are commonly found by detectorists as its use was widespread in this country but tin objects are encountered less frequently, as it was more often alloyed with other metals, most notably with copper to form bronze. Tin was also alloyed with lead in various proportions to form pewter. The term 'pewter' actually covers a variety of compositions. Roman pewter was an alloy generally containing anything between about 50% and 95% tin alloyed with lead. Medieval pewter could have been 'fine metal' (tin alloyed with up to 3% copper), 'lay metal' (tin alloyed with anything up to about 25% lead); or an alloy similar to Roman pewter. Modern pewter, also known as Britannia metal, is an alloy of tin with about 8% antimony and 2% copper.

Pewter has been made since Roman times and was mainly used to make vessels and tableware and was at the height of its popularity around AD 1700. Most pewter objects were cast in the first instance, but further finishing would be done as the object was turned on a lathe.

Lead, tin and pewter objects were sometimes made to be used in conjunction with other materials; for example, the strips of lead, or cames, between panels of window glass or lead 'plugs' used to repair holes in ceramic vessels. Lead and its alloys were also frequently used as a solder on other metal artefacts because of their low melting point.

Iron

Iron seems to have been first introduced to the British Isles around the sixth or seventh centuries BC. By the fifth century BC it had become the metal of preference for the manufacture of tools and weapons in particular, largely because its ore sources were widely available across most of Britain and because it was less likely to shatter than copper alloys when worked. The earliest finds of iron in Europe suggest that initially it was a rare and valuable metal; for example, it was used as a decorative inlay on bronze razors in Denmark at the end of the Bronze Age. By the end of the Iron Age (the middle of the first century AD) objects being made of iron included swords and scabbards, spearheads, knives, socketed axes, wheel tyres, chains, razors and fire-dogs. By the Roman period, a wide range of objects were being made of iron – ploughs, nails, window grilles, bed frames, armour, and tools of all descriptions. By the Anglo-Saxon period, iron was widely used for weapons and tools as well as for personal items such as buckles or the pins on copper alloy brooches.

Iron has the highest melting point of the metals used in antiquity, and the temperatures required to melt it were not achievable in antiquity in Britain. Once the technology to produce strong reducing conditions in a furnace had been mastered, iron could be smelted from its ores. The use of charcoal, rather than ordinary wood, enabled early ironworkers to achieve the right conditions. If pure iron ore was used, iron could be extracted at temperatures as low as 800°C, well below its melting point of 1540°C. The temperature in the furnace needed to be high enough for the non-metal part of the ore, i.e. the slag, to drain away, leaving behind the metal as a solid spongy lump or bloom. Depending on the nature of the impurities in the ore, temperatures as high as 1150°C might be needed. The next stage in the process would be forging, consisting of a cycle of heating and hammering to literally squeeze out as much of any slag that remained in the bloom as possible, leaving the iron behind.

The iron produced in this way is referred to as wrought iron. By more hammering (forging), both hot and cold, the smith formed the wrought iron into objects. The iron was seldom absolutely pure and its working properties would be affected by impurities, particularly phosphorus and carbon. Phosphorus made the iron harder and stronger but also more brittle when cold worked. If carbon was present, alloyed with the iron to form steel, a very hard iron could be produced by cycles of hammering and quenching (rapidly cooling from about 720°C).

Heating iron in contact with carbon, in a reducing atmosphere, which could happen during smelting or forging if charcoal was used, would eventually produce a steel, or iron-carbon, alloy. With the technology available in antiquity, achieving deliberate carburization through the whole thickness of a bloom would have been very difficult and time consuming. However, the hardness of a blade could be considerably improved by just raising the carbon content of its working edges. One way this was done was to weld a carburized strip onto the cutting edge of the wrought iron object.

When in antiquity smiths first deliberately produced carburized-iron or steel, as opposed to it occurring accidentally during smelting or forging, is still a matter of debate amongst archaeologists and historical metallurgists. By the early Roman period (the first century AD) however, we have enough evidence from surviving tools and weapons to suggest that smiths were deliberately adding steel edges to their products.

By the end of the first millennium BC, blacksmiths had mastered plating iron artefacts with copper alloys and by the Roman period, they were able to inlay iron scabbards and sheaths with intricate designs in silver. Iron objects were also sometimes decorated with enamel and niello inlay.

Summary

This chapter has described the various types of metals which detectorists may encounter and how they were made into objects. The next chapter looks in more detail at the different corrosion products which might be seen on excavated objects, and also provides information on where the 'original surfaces' of these objects might be located.

3 Corrosion and 'original surfaces'

Why metals corrode

Everyday examples of metal corrosion can be seen when iron objects turn rusty or silver tarnishes. Most metals corrode in the presence of water and air (oxygen), which means that they begin to revert to their natural mineral (or ore) forms. The extent of this corrosion depends on many factors, and determines that the appearance and properties of an ancient metal object, after excavation, are likely to be very different to those of the original object.

The tendency for a metal to corrode depends upon the amount of energy (heat) that was needed to extract the pure metal from the ore in the first place. The more energy required, the more unstable the pure metal form. Thus iron is the most unstable metal, because it is the most difficult to extract from its ore, whereas gold is the most stable, since it does not corrode, and occurs in nature in its pure form.

The order of stability of the metals of antiquity is:

GOLD	SILVER	COPPER	LEAD	TIN	IRON

⟵——————————————————————————————⟶

most noble	most base
most stable	most unstable
least likely to corrode	most likely to corrode

Stability of metals after excavation

If the burial environment of a metal object remains unchanged for a long time, the rate of corrosion may slow and almost stop. The layers of corrosion help to prevent water and oxygen (both essential agents for corrosion to proceed) from gaining access to the underlying metal. Once a buried object is removed from the soil, there is a sudden and drastic change to its environment which can reverse any stability. The change can cause corrosion of the metal to start again or alter the form of the corrosion products. These changes can destroy an object.

A change in the colour or form of a metal object and its corrosion may indicate that it is no longer stable. An example of this on copper alloys is the appearance or spread, after excavation, of bright green powdery corrosion (a form of copper chloride), often referred to as 'bronze disease' – although it is not contagious. The activation of corrosion is especially dependent upon environmental conditions (humidity, temperature and pollutants).

Where is the 'original surface'?

All the different metals of antiquity and their alloys corrode in different ways, and the extent of the corrosion can also vary depending on the burial environment. When presented with a corroded object, the conservator and archaeologist want to discover the original shape of the object, and where this surface is located within the corrosion.

The 'original surface' is not necessarily at the surface of any surviving bright metal, but most often lies preserved within the corrosion layers, in particular for corroded iron and copper alloy objects. It can be extremely difficult to recognise the often subtle changes in the corrosion, which indicate the location of the 'original surface'. Also the overlying layers of corrosion may be considerably harder than the level of corrosion which preserves the shape and detail of an object's original surface. Thus indiscriminate cleaning to remove corrosion could completely remove/destroy this 'original surface' (see chapters 7 and 8), and perhaps damage any traces of gilding, inlay, niello and enamels that may also be preserved, or hidden, by corrosion layers.

Patination

In antiquity, not all metal objects were intended to be the colour of the bright clean shiny metal. Then, as now, metals were sometimes deliberately coloured or patinated. For example, silver and iron were sometimes blackened and this colour/patina was deliberately induced by controlled corrosion of the metal. Deliberate patination or colouring can be impossible to distinguish from burial corrosion products by analysis, and the possibility of its occurrence on an artefact is yet another reason for not removing or changing the appearance of corrosion on metal objects.

Gold

Gold is the most stable of the metals used in antiquity. Pure gold does not corrode when buried. Less stable metals with which it was alloyed (silver or copper), or to which the gold was applied as decoration, may corrode, however, and can completely hide the original appearance of the gold.

Having said that, if an object looks like gold when excavated, then it probably *is* gold, but there are exceptions to this. For example, in some water-logged burial conditions, objects can become covered in deposits of a form of iron sulphide (iron pyrites) more commonly known as 'fool's gold'. Certain burial conditions can cause copper alloy artefacts to gradually dissolve, with what remains of the object, when found, often having a bright yellow surface which could be mistaken for gold.

The 'original surface' of a gold artefact will be at the level of any remaining uncorroded gold. If a base metal artefact has a gold surface or gilded decoration, this will often have overlying copper corrosion products obscuring the gold.

Silver

Even pure silver will corrode in most burial environments in the British Isles. The presence of impurities and/or other metals in the alloy, together with the particular conditions of the burial environment, will determine the nature, colour and extent of the corrosion. Corrosion products may completely cover and hide the bright silver surface.

Surface corrosion layers on excavated silver can be:

- **Black** & smooth – due to a corrosion layer or patina of silver sulphide. Black silver sulphide may be tarnish or it may have been applied in antiquity as a deliberate patina. It may also be niello – a deliberately applied compound with the same composition as the corrosion product. Such deliberate original patination can be impossible to distinguish from environmental or burial corrosion because the compounds produced are the same.

- **Grey white** – (which takes on a dull lilac hue very shortly after removal from the ground), dull and waxy, and can vary from a smooth patina to a distorted crust. This corrosion product is mainly silver chloride, also known as 'horn silver'. It is most likely to occur on purer silver. The 'original surface' may be within the corrosion or just beneath it, depending on how far corrosion has progressed.

- **Green** – due to a copper (carbonate) corrosion crust. This occurs on silver alloyed with copper i.e. base silver (good examples of this are base silver coins of the Roman period). A good silver surface may be preserved under the green corrosion (**colour plate 1**). If the object originally had just an applied silver surface coating, traces of this silvering may only survive as 'floating' flecks within green copper corrosion.

The presence of copper in base silver may be sufficient to preserve organic remains (textile, leather, wood etc.) which might originally have been in contact with, or part of, the object. For example, traces of textile may survive on the backs of brooches.

Copper alloys

Copper alloy objects can be found with a range of corrosion products depending on the composition of the alloy and on the burial conditions. The physical condition and appearance of corrosion products are also effected by the environmental conditions in which they form.

Surface corrosion layers on excavated copper alloy objects can be:

- **Red/brown** (a copper oxide) – this layer usually develops on bright copper alloy surfaces in the air. When buried in an oxygen-rich soil, this red copper oxide will continue to develop on the surface of the metal, followed by green copper carbonate.

- **Green** (a copper carbonate) – this forms over the red oxide layer resulting in a characteristic, layered corrosion structure. Under conditions where corrosion develops slowly, dark green corrosion forms with good preservation of surface detail. Rapid corrosion activity, however, can produce thick, green porous corrosion, which may retain the 'original surface' within the layers. In very aggressive conditions, the 'original surface' can be destroyed, together with any remaining metal core: conservators tend to describe such an object as completely mineralised (**colour plate 2**).

- The hard warts and blisters that may disrupt the otherwise smooth surface of an object are the result of localised, intense corrosion activity. A **pale green** (copper chloride) powdery corrosion, underneath a compact surface or inside pits, indicates active corrosion, or 'bronze disease'.

Copper alloy corrosion products can also be:

- **White/grey** (oxides) – these are due to preferential corrosion of the other metals in the alloy. For example, lead or tin-rich copper alloys may have white/grey corrosion products.

- **Black** (copper sulphides) – these may form where there are sulphides in the burial environment, for example in waterlogged conditions, where oxygen is scarce. Black corrosion on copper alloys may also be a different type of copper oxide – but it is more likely to be a copper sulphide.

It is possible for copper alloys to be found looking still bright and shiny, though often with a pitted surface, despite hundreds, if not thousands, of years of burial. Objects in this condition may come from waterlogged contexts, where oxygen was scarce. The pitted appearance often seen on such artefacts is due to non-copper metals in the alloy dissolving out from the surface.

After burial and excavation, whatever its appearance, a copper alloy artefact will be much more fragile than when it was originally made. Corrosion can penetrate deep into the object and weaken its internal structure. Some objects may be totally corroded or mineralised, while other artefacts may still contain a substantial metal core.

The location of the 'original surface' of a copper alloy artefact will depend on the type and extent of corrosion. There may be a protective patina of copper carbonates overlying a layer of powdery, lighter green copper chlorides. The denser patina will often preserve the surface detail. Unstable copper alloys will display flaking layers or blisters and pits. The level of the 'original surface' may be lost by corrosion or obscured by corrosion blisters. Sometimes the detail of the original surface may be within the red copper oxide layer, or at its junction with the overlying green carbonate layer.

Lead and tin

The most common lead corrosion products are:

- **whitish-brown** lead carbonates.

- **pale brown or whitish-grey** lead oxides. Lead oxides can also be **red** or **yellow-brown** depending on the conditions under which they form.

- **dark grey-black** lead sulphide invariably forms on lead objects buried in waterlogged soils.

The lead carbonates, oxides and sulphides can all form protective layers that slow down the subsequent corrosion of an object. The original form of an object may therefore be easily identified, but various factors can reduce the protective nature of these layers leading to disfiguring corrosion 'warts' and deeply cracked objects.

In acid soils, lead objects can become very corroded, particularly in the presence of organic acids. The corrosion products formed are easily soluble in water and so will be leached away, enabling corrosion to continue until eventually almost nothing remains of the artefact.

On tin objects, a protective corrosion layer of tin oxide often forms. It may form a smooth even protective patina but can also be found as more disfiguring 'warts' on the surface. Sometimes, tin objects will be in a more disrupted state, with deep cracks present. The colour of tin oxide corrosion can vary from black to grey-brown to white depending on the type of oxide that has formed.

Pewter will usually have a mixture of lead and tin corrosion products, although the exact nature of the corrosion will be dependent on the proportions of lead and tin present. Both pewter and tin objects can be brittle when found, whereas lead objects will often retain some flexibility unless they are extensively corroded. Objects made of lead, or pewter containing a very high proportion of lead, are commonly distorted during burial because lead is so soft and pliable.

Due to the way in which lead and tin and pewter corrode, it is generally fair to say that the corrosion products themselves often give the best indication of the original shape of the object and the form of its surface. Thus, any attempt to remove the corrosion products down to a sound metal layer will usually result in the object's original shape and surface detail being lost, along with any information that it may have contained.

Iron

Iron can corrode very quickly, and layered bulky corrosion products often develop. The most common iron corrosion products are:

- **Orange-brown** (iron hydroxides) – this corrosion is usually the outermost surface corrosion layer on iron excavated from aerobic (oxygen-rich) soils. These can form a thick layer on the surface of the artefact completely obscuring its original shape.

- **Dark grey-black** (iron oxide) – this usually develops beneath the orange brown outer corrosion layer.

A sound core of unaltered iron may survive within the object, or the metal may be completely converted to iron oxide. In some burial conditions the way in which the iron corrodes leaves a void at the centre of the object (**colour plate 3**). In extreme cases, the 'object' may only exist as a hollow cast within a thick crust of corrosion and soil.

On the other hand, burial conditions may protect the object and corrosion may be minimal. The excavated object may only have a light covering of corrosion products. For example, objects recovered from waterlogged conditions, such as beneath a riverbed, may have a thin covering of **black** and/or **golden** iron sulphides, with considerable surface detail still visible.

A **blue** (iron phosphate) corrosion product may form on iron buried in a phospate-rich environment. Iron from very chalky soils can also be only lightly corroded and the general form of the object will often be obvious.

The 'original surface' of a corroded iron object can be difficult to locate. Generally the boundary between the dark grey oxide and the outer layer of orange-brown corrosion products is taken as representing the position of an object's 'original surface', although it is not always easy to determine.

Mineral preserved organic remains

Many metal objects, used in antiquity, also had organic parts. For example, an iron sword might have had a bone handle (**colour plate 4**) and been kept in a leather scabbard. In most burial conditions found in the UK, the organic parts of such a composite object are unlikely to survive.

However, traces of these perishable organic materials often do survive, where they were lying closest to the metal. For instance, wood can be preserved in sockets of spears or around the tangs of knives, and textiles can survive on the backs of brooches. These organic materials are preserved by the metal corrosion products.

On iron objects, traces of organic material can survive as impressions or casts in the corrosion. There may no longer be any wood or leather left, but the form of the organic material still remains from replacement by the metal's corrosion products (**colour plates 6-8**). On copper alloy objects, the toxic nature of copper corrosion will inhibit bacteria and mould growth, and this can prevent the deterioration of organic materials close to the metal (**colour plate 5**).

Organic materials in all these forms are often referred to by conservators as 'mineral preserved organics'.

Summary

This chapter concludes the section on background information. An overview has been presented of different corrosion products which might be seen on different metals and alloys used in the past, and where 'original surfaces' might be located.

Part II of the book provides practical advice on how finders should deal with objects in the field (chapter 4), and then in the home and the long term (chapter 5 onwards).

PART II: PRACTICAL ADVICE
4 In the field

Anyone who has ever been metal detecting or field walking will know that conditions can vary greatly from one excursion to another. A huge number of factors can come into play with regard to how successful or otherwise a day is perceived. The weather, the underlying soil conditions, the presence or otherwise of stubble on cropped arable land, whether or not land has been ploughed recently – all have their part to play.

The above factors will affect the enjoyment of a metal detecting trip, and also the amount of material which is recovered either by eye (what detectorists call 'eyes only' finds) or with a metal detecting device. For instance, if conditions are very dry, a metal detector may pick up fewer signals than if there has been a light shower of rain the night before. Wet and darker soil may mean that pieces of flint or pottery are easier to spot with the naked eye.

The other factor which comes into play is the nature of the site being surveyed, i.e. what the underlying archaeology consists of. This can vary from a previously undiscovered high status Roman villa site, to a mass of Victorian rubbish spread over a field.

However, disregarding the circumstances surrounding the discovery of finds by metal detectorists, once objects have been removed from the soil, finders have a responsibility to look after them properly. This chapter sets out to provide advice on how finders can behave responsibly in the field to ensure that objects are treated with the necessary care and respect.

Sorting finds in the field

Many professional archaeologists and conservators would say that EVERY artefact recovered, regardless of date or the material which the artefact is made of, should be treated in the same manner. But even on professionally run archae-ological sites, on-the-spot decisions are made about how objects are handled. 'Bulk finds', for example pieces of broken pottery and animal bone, will probably be placed into a plastic tray with a common context number, which means that after processing it is possible to work out where on the archaeological site they came from. 'Small finds', on the other hand, which can be anything from coins and brooches to a worked bone pin, will be treated rather differently. Small finds will usually be plotted 'three dimensionally', so that their exact position on the site can be established; and they will certainly be given a unique find number, and bagged and tagged separately from the other material found in their context.

Metal detectorists tend to deal with material which has been dragged out of its archaeological context into the ploughsoil (assuming that the detecting is taking place on ploughed land). This means that both types of find are all mixed up together. Unlike on an archaeological site, where it is usually possible to recognise different dating phases, material in ploughsoil can come from all historical periods, with it being perfectly possible to find a prehistoric flint axe lying alongside a penny of Elizabeth I. The situation is even more complicated than this, because it will not just be archaeological material which is present in the topsoil, but a vast quantity of what detectorists refer to as 'junk'. This can be anything from a bolt which came loose from a tractor in the 1950s, to an empty can of cola dropped only last week (**1**).

The range of material which detectorists might recover is thus extremely varied, but tends to be skewed in the direction of the modern junk. Therefore the first thing that metal detectorists have to decide when they find something is simple: is the object modern junk, or is it of possible archaeological importance? We would provide the following advice on this:

- If the finder is 100% CERTAIN that the object is 'modern junk', these objects can be placed in a bag or pouch and later discarded. More experienced detectorists will be able to tell such items much more quickly than a beginner.

- If the finder is NOT 100% CERTAIN that the object is 'modern junk', these objects should be treated in the same manner as objects known to be of archaeological significance.

If an object is thought to be of archaeological importance, the advice given below should be followed.

Objects of archaeological importance include the following categories of find:

- non-coin objects made before about 1650 of any type of material (anything from prehistoric worked flints to medieval shoe buckles), although ideally, finds of the late seventeenth and eighteenth centuries should also be treated as archaeologically significant;

- all gold and silver objects regardless of date, particularly as these may be subject to the Treasure Act (Appendix 1);

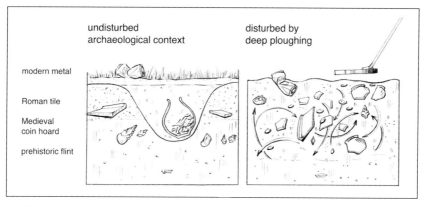

1 *The picture on the left shows some undisturbed archaeology prior to deep ploughing. A pit for the deposition of a medieval coin hoard has been dug into Roman and prehistoric archaeological deposits. On the right, deep ploughing has mixed up all the archaeological material, breaking the container of the coin hoard and spreading the contents and fragments in the process. This means that if any detecting occurs, finds discovered could come from any of the historical periods covered by the finds.* Copyright Kate Morton

- all coins made before about 1660 (the beginning of the reign of Charles II), although ideally, coins of the late seventeenth and eighteenth century should also be considered as archaeologically significant.

Below are described ways in which metal detector users should treat these categories of artefact.

Finds which should ONLY be excavated with professional help

There are some types of archaeological find which should only be excavated with professional help, and finders are strongly advised to contact their local museum, archaeologist or finds liaison officer if they make such discoveries (see Appendix 3). Such finds include hoards, fragile objects and objects found in association with organic components. Proper archaeological excavation will record information about the context of the find, which is a vital part of understanding why the object/s have been found in that particular place, and will also carefully excavate and record the find itself. A good example of this is the Hoxne treasure, the largest hoard of late Roman gold and silver ever discovered in Britain, which was excavated by professional archaeologists after the finder very sensibly realised the importance of his find and stopped removing objects from the soil. Another example is a deposit of Iron Age metalwork from Essendon in Hertfordshire (**colour plate 9**).

If a coin or metalwork hoard has been discovered, especially one that is contained within a vessel, finders should stop excavating the find immediately, back fill the hole, discreetly mark the spot so that they know where to go back to, and go and get help. Professional archaeologists would investigate the surroundings of a hoard in order to understand the context of the find, for example to see if there is evidence for burial in a pit or a pottery container.

Whenever possible, a hoard would be lifted as one, in its original container if it survives (**colour plate 10**). Even where the container may not be visible to the naked eye, minute traces of it may survive that may only be apparent on closer examination under a microscope. The original container, with its contents undisturbed, would be packed into a rigid container, padded with 'Jiffy' foam, and covered with polythene sheeting. When a hoard is not in an original container, the objects would probably still be lifted as a group within their surrounding soil. The latter may not only contain important evidence, but would also act as a support for fragile objects. The objects plus surrounding soil would then be placed in a rigid container as above. Once back in the laboratory, the archaeological conservator can then carefully excavate the block in an environment which is much safer and controllable than the open field, giving the finds a much better chance of being properly excavated and conserved (**colour plate 11**).

Other types of find likely to benefit from professional help are those which are fragile or those with associated material, such as organic components (e.g. wood or bone). These sorts of finds may need to be lifted with additional support. A professional conservator would use a support, which could be as simple as a sheet of rigid plastic or cardboard slid underneath the object, or something more complex. Bandaging with plaster of Paris or a casting bandage might be used to lift very fragile finds (e.g. a cremation urn). A layer of 'cling film' or aluminium foil might be used as a separating layer to protect the artefact from the lifting material. Often the soil itself is used to provide a good support until the artefact can be 'excavated' in relative comfort, indoors. **In all the cases described above, finders are strongly advised to seek the help of a professional archaeologist.**

Retrieving finds without professional help

Assuming that finds made in the field are neither 'modern junk' nor the types of find which should only be excavated by professional archaeologists, then detectorists should follow the advice below to recover finds of archaeological significance.

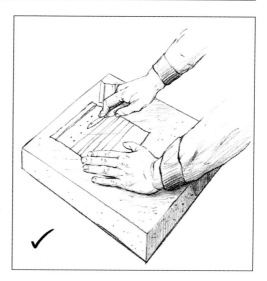

2 *Good practice: small holes should be made in polythene finds bags before a detecting trip. Here a penknife is being used and some soft foam padding. Alternatively, a row of nails knocked into a small piece of wood could be used to pierce a number of bags at the same time.*
Copyright Kate Morton

Step 1: what to take into the field

The first thing which should be considered even before setting off on a detecting or fieldwalking trip is what to take. Below is a list of things which should be taken in order to ensure that any objects found are well looked after and are less likely to become damaged. (It is assumed that detectorists are aware that they must obtain permission from the landowner before searching and must not detect on protected archaeological sites. More information can be found in Appendix 1.)

The bare minimum of things which should be taken are:

- clear, perforated, polythene bags of different sizes (the best ones are the self-seal type). Bags can be pierced with a few holes at the top with a sharp object such as a penknife or nail (**2**). Alternatively, to save time, a number of bags can be pierced by hammering nails through a short piece of wood and pressing these through a stack of bags placed on a soft surface such as foam padding.
- labels (ideally polythene ones, which do not deteriorate, for example 'Tyvek' labels).
- permanent pens (which will not run in the rain or if they get wet from the object).
- sealable polythene (for example, 'Tupperware' or 'Stewart') boxes with well-fitting lids to store groups of finds.

Consideration should also be given to taking:

- small 'crystal' boxes, which are made of clear hard polystyrene.
- 'jiffy' foam padding and bubble wrap (also made from polythene).

All these items can be very easily obtained from the list of suppliers provided at the back of this guide (Appendix 3), and many can also be purchased in your local high street (certainly permanent marker pens, tupperware boxes and polythene bags). See also the list of packing materials in **Table 3**.

Step 2: after archaeological objects have been retrieved

When an object is discovered in the soil, its shape and surface may be hidden by earth. This earth may hide the fragile nature of the artefact but may also form a support for the object. Years of burial will have caused changes that will have weakened the physical structure of the find. The object's surface may also be disrupted by corrosion. To minimise any damage, it is important to avoid removing the earth immediately – it is much better to get it home first before attempting to remove surrounding soil.

It should also be borne in mind that soil and corrosion on the surface of an object may contain evidence about how the artefact was used. For example, what appear to be just darker areas of soil may in fact be all that remains of a leather purse or wrapping.

Below is a summary list of good practice and bad practice for objects retrieved in the field. Once again, this list applies to objects of potential archae- ological importance, not 'junk' as described in the introduction to this chapter.

Good practice in the field

✓ Store each object **individually** in a sealable, perforated polythene finds bag.

✓ Write on each bag where the object was found, and the day's date **before you put the object inside** (not the probable date of the object itself!), and/or use a finds label placed inside the bag. Findspots can be plotted by using the increasingly popular (and relatively inexpensive) handheld GPS (Global Positioning System) devices (**3**), or by reference to an Ordnance Survey map (see Appendix 2). Even reference to a suitable landmark is better than nothing. If a note is made of a findspot separately (e.g. in a notebook), make sure that it is possible to tie the find to the findspot, e.g. by using a running sequence of numbers.

✓ If the object has been discovered in a waterlogged environment, it is very important to keep the object wet *and* keep it separate from 'dry' or damp finds. Such objects should be stored in **unperforated** polythene bags, and advice from a professional conservator should be sought as soon as possible (Appendix 3).

✓ Put all the day's finds, each in separate bags, in a 'Tupperware' box or even better in individual 'crystal' boxes with foam padding and then in a 'Tupperware' box. Ensure that the box is well padded, either with foam padding or bubble wrap, in order that finds do not rattle around. Bubble wrap should **not** be in direct contact with the objects themselves, as the bubbles can sometimes mark objects (**4**).

✓ Ensure that any holes dug are backfilled with the soil removed by digging.

1 *Base silver snake rings from the Snettisham jeweller's hoard, Norfolk. The silver nature of the rings was completely obscured by copper corrosion (left). After careful cleaning, the silver nature of one of the rings is revealed (right). Note that these objects would have to be declared treasure under the Treasure Act.*
Copyright The British Museum

2 *Cross section of a copper-alloy dagger blade from the ancient Near East. Although this is not a British find, it demonstrates the layered manner in which copper corrosion develops. The main layers from the outside in, on the lower cross section, are: green copper carbonate (malachite), red copper oxide (cuprite), then a thin sliver of all that is left of the original metal. In the upper cross section there is no metal at the centre at all — just an empty void. The blue copper carbonate (azurite) is rarely seen on British material.*
Copyright The British Museum

3 *Cross section of an iron tyre from Wetwang, East Yorkshire, dating to the Iron Age. The corrosion has been so severe that no original metal survives, but the shape of the object is at least preserved in the black and orange corrosion products. This provided enough evidence to help archaeologists understand how the chariot was constructed.* Copyright The British Museum

4 *The hilt of an iron sword with part of a well-preserved bone handle. The preservation of organics has been possible because the item was found in waterlogged conditions where anaerobic (oxygen-free) conditions meant that the organic component (bone) did not biodegrade.* Copyright The British Museum

5 *Mineral preserved textile wrapping around an Iron Age copper-alloy torc from Snettisham, Norfolk. The textile has been preserved because the toxic nature of the copper corrosion salts has prevented the textile from degrading.*
Copyright The British Museum

6 *Mineral preserved textile on an iron object; textile fibres have been completely replaced by the iron corrosion products.*
Copyright The British Museum

7 *Mineral preserved organic remains of wood and leather on the back of an Anglo-Saxon iron shield boss. This object has been cleaned, but before this happened, the object may have looked as if it was just covered in powdery soil and corrosion.*
Copyright The British Museum

8 *Under magnification, the wood and leather remains of the shield preserved on the back of the shield boss (**colour plate 7**) are clearly visible. The wood appears as a brown colour, the leather as powdery yellow.*
Copyright The British Museum

9 *Excavation of a hoard of Iron Age metalwork in Hertfordshire. The site was originally discovered by a metal detectorist, who contacted archaeologists allowing the hoard to be properly excavated. The detectorist, archaeologist and conservator are all working together here.* Copyright The British Museum

10 *The hoard of Iron Age metalwork (**colour plate 9**), being lifted in a block. The block consists of polyurethene foam, which provides protection and support for the objects being lifted en masse.* Copyright The British Museum

11 *The hoard of Iron Age metalwork (**colour plate 10**) after excavation in the laboratory by a professional conservator, revealing a number of iron spearheads and swords, lying on the remains of a copper-alloy shield.*
Copyright The British Museum

12 *Good practice: storage materials for objects. Shown are objects packed with 'Plastazote' foam padding inside a crystal box (bottom left), an object padded with a bed of acid free tissue inside a crystal box (bottom right). Also shown are sachets of silica gel, a clear polythene box with acid free tissue padding, a relative humidity strip and a thermohygrometer that records temperature and RH levels inside the box.*
Copyright Celia Honeycombe

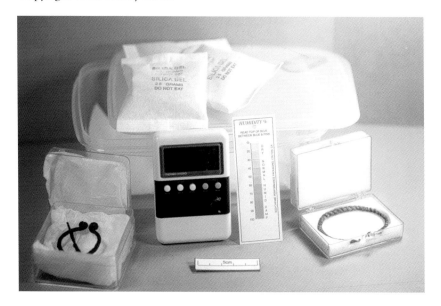

13 *Good practice: recently excavated finds packed in labelled polythene bags with additional 'Plastazote' foam for support. The bags have been pierced at the top to allow air to circulate.* Copyright The British Museum

14 *Signs of trouble. A close-up of an iron object shows spots of active corrosion in the form of orange liquid droplets known as 'weeping'.* Copyright The British Museum

15 *Signs of trouble. Bright orange powdery areas of active corrosion are visible on this iron object. The corrosion has occurred inside the object and expanded, which has caused flaking and pitting of the surface.* Copyright The British Museum

16 *Signs of trouble. This lead token is very unstable, some parts of the edge have broken off and the visible white powder is active corrosion.*
Copyright The British Museum

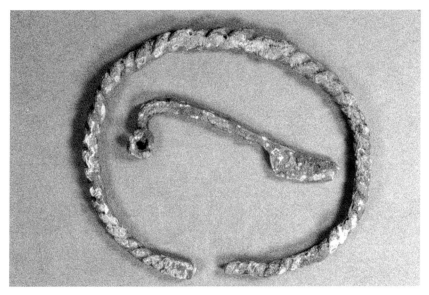

17 *Signs of trouble. Roman bracelet and bow brooch in poor condition. Both show the blisters, pits and powdery green corrosion which is typical of 'bronze disease'.* Copyright Celia Honeycombe

18 *Signs of trouble. Here active spots of green 'bronze disease' are clearly visible on the surface of a copper-alloy object.* Copyright The British Museum

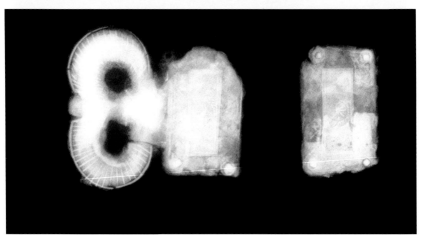

22 *Three-quarters cleaned Anglo-Saxon silver-gilt brooch with garnet inlay. This has been manually cleaned after the corrosion was softened gently with a solvent.* Copyright The British Museum

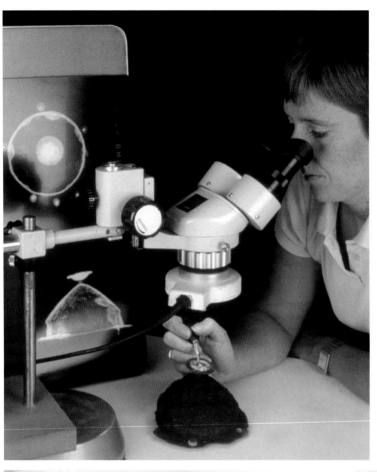

23 *(opposite above) A conservator examining an Anglo-Saxon iron shield boss under a microscope with the help of an x-radiograph.* Copyright The British Museum

24 *(opposite below) A range of small hand tools used by a conservator. These include a puffer to blow dust away, tweezers, scalpel blades, brushes and gloves. These are all used for the skilled manual cleaning of objects under magnification.* Copyright Celia Honeycombe

25 *(above) A silver coin which has been half cleaned with a glass bristle brush. Scratches can be seen on the surface where the cleaning has been too harsh. This demonstrates that even 'good' cleaning methods can cause damage if the tool in use is not being applied correctly.* Copyright Celia Honeycombe

26 *(below) A conservator using a pneumatic pen and a microscope to reveal the original surface of a copper-alloy object. Gloves are worn to protect the hands, and a mask is worn to protect the conservator from any dust created during the work.* Copyright The British Museum

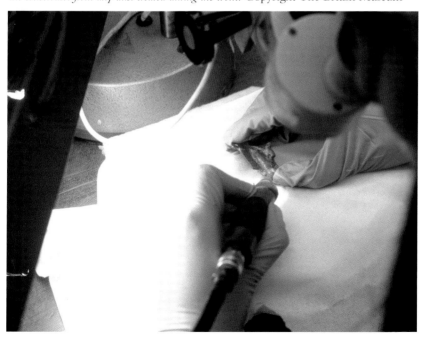

27 *Fragment of a Roman copper alloy object, half cleaned with a cotton wool swab dampened with Industrial Methylated Spirits (IMS).* Copyright Celia Honeycombe

28 *Bad practice: treatments to be avoided include table salt, denture cleaner (see* **colour plate 29***) and disinfectant. Table salt is the worst thing for metal objects to be exposed to: the damage caused by immersion in a saline (salt) solution can clearly be seen (second from left).* Copyright Celia Honeycombe

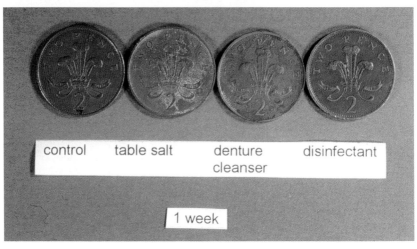

control   table salt   denture cleanser   disinfectant

1 week

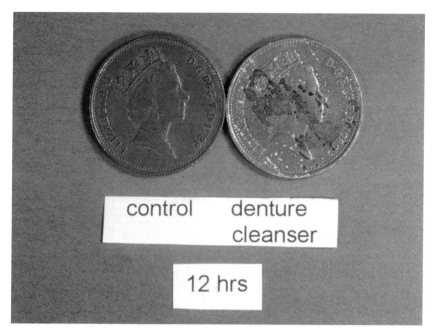

29 *Bad practice: treatments to be avoided include denture cleaning fluid. The coin on the right quite clearly shows how damaging these substances can be to metal objects.* Copyright Celia Honeycombe

30 *Coatings and lacquers. This shows the protective properties and the potential damage of different wax coatings. The coin on the left has no coating and may develop pits of corrosion in damp conditions. The middle coin has been protected by a stable wax, in this case 'Renaissance Wax'. The coin on the right has been coated with boot polish, which is very harmful to metals; as can be seen, corrosion spots have developed due to unstable constituents in the polish.* Copyright Celia Honeycombe

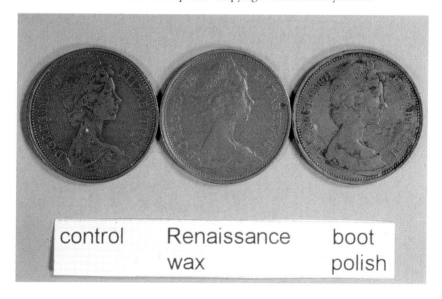

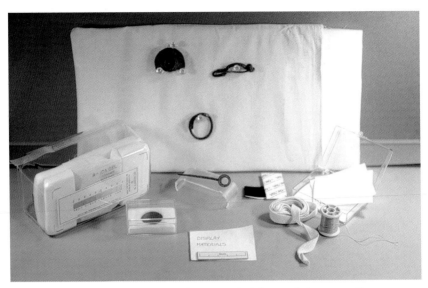

31 *A variety of good and stable display materials. These include cotton calico, polystyrene boxes with 'Plastazote' foam padding, and one box with silica gel, pins with plastic coverings and 'Velcro'.* Copyright Celia Honeycombe

32 *Good and bad mounting methods for coins. The left coin has been correctly mounted using stainless steel pins covered with plastic catheter tubing. The right coin has been badly mounted with bare pins that abrade the surface and are possible sites for galvanic corrosion, which occurs when two dissimilar metals are in direct contact.* Copyright Celia Honeycombe

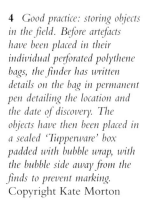

3 *Good practice: taking a GPS reading in the field. This is a relatively 'high tech' way of recording the location of a find; taking a grid reference from a map (or at least recording the farm name) is a habit all finders should get into when making discoveries.*
Copyright Kate Morton

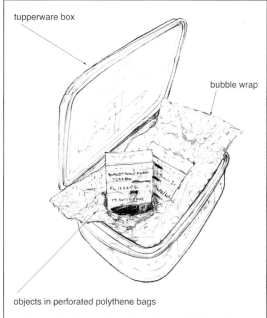

tupperware box

bubble wrap

objects in perforated polythene bags

4 *Good practice: storing objects in the field. Before artefacts have been placed in their individual perforated polythene bags, the finder has written details on the bag in permanent pen detailing the location and the date of discovery. The objects have then been placed in a sealed 'Tupperware' box padded with bubble wrap, with the bubble side away from the finds to prevent marking.*
Copyright Kate Morton

5 *Bad practice in the field. The finder is rubbing his find on his sleeve, not recommended, and has not bothered to fill in holes from previous discoveries. He is also detecting on pasture, which is also not recommended, as the archaeology may be otherwise undisturbed. He is also not bothering to note where he is finding things.* Copyright Kate Morton

Bad practice in the field

✗ Finders should not be tempted to give objects a good rub on their sleeve (**5**), or to pick away at the immediate surrounding soil with their hands. There may be important evidence about the object that is being destroyed in eagerness to find out what the object is.

✗ Finds should not be washed in the nearest river, for the same reasons as rubbing finds on a sleeve (**6**).

✗ Finds should not be placed in bags with other objects or stuffed in pockets.

✗ Finds should not be wrapped in tissue paper or newspaper, or put in cardboard boxes or brown paper envelopes – see above and **Table 3** (chapter 4) for suitable materials.

6 *Bad practice: washing finds in the nearest river is not recommended. Important information about the object may be washed away in the process, and the object is also likely to be damaged by such harsh treatment.* Copyright Kate Morton

Summary

If the advice given above is followed, the following situation should be reached:

- 'Junk' can be amalgamated and discarded at a later date. Some detectorists will place a pile of junk in a marked corner of a field, in order that it can be reviewed just in case it contains finds which were not recognised in the first instance.
- Any material discovered which is very fragile or of obvious archaeological importance as an assemblage is left undisturbed until a professional archaeologist can be contacted.
- All objects of potential and definite archaeological importance are individually bagged and have information with them about when and where they were found.
- Groups of finds are safely placed in suitable containers which ensure that no damage occurs to them when transported home.
- Any waterlogged material is kept wet until a professional conservator can be contacted for advice.

In the next chapter, how finds should be dealt with at home is discussed.

5 At home: first steps, storage and signs of trouble

The good work of successfully transporting finds home from the field, without damage, can easily be undone by impatience and overeagerness to find out what has been discovered. One of the first things that detectorists might do is wash finds under the kitchen tap: **THIS IS NOT RECOMMENDED** (**7**). Soil and corrosion adhering to a fragile object may not only be holding it together, but may also contain evidence of how an object was made or used – which could all too easily be washed down the drain!

This chapter provides advice on how to deal with finds that have just been brought home from the field under the following headings:

    Step 1: Handling objects
    Step 2: What is it made of?
    Step 3: Is it treasure?
    Step 4: To dry or not to dry?
    Step 5: Packing and storing finds
    Step 6: Spotting signs of trouble

The aim of these first steps is to get an idea of what the object might be made of (without cleaning it), and on the basis of its condition to put it into a storage environment which will at least minimize – if not prevent – corrosion and deterioration, before the object can be properly examined and treated. This chapter also includes how to spot signs of trouble – changes in the appearance of an object that indicate that it is actively corroding and what to do about it.

It is strongly recommended that, if possible, a special area is set aside for working with finds (**8**). Such an area need not be large but should include:

- a clean table or desk with chair.
- a sheet of foam (e.g. 'Plastazote') or padding on the table to provide soft support for objects.
- a good light (from a window, or a desk lamp) – but not direct sunlight.
- an electricity supply.
- a bench magnifying glass or ideally a binocular microscope.
- storage (for instance, drawers) for packing materials, tools, objects, papers, chemicals.
- a nearby source of water.

7 *Bad practice: washing finds under the tap is not recommended for the vast majority of finds. Damage may be done to the find in the process, and important information about the object may be washed away for ever. Our finder should also not be reaching for a scrubbing brush, as this can badly damage delicate objects.* Copyright Kate Morton

The area should also be:

- safe from children and pets!
- away from eating, drinking and smoking areas.

Step 1: Handling objects

A lot of damage can be caused to metal objects by poor handling – the most common example is the accidental dropping of artefacts which can result in breakage. Whenever possible, objects should be handled over a soft surface and the whole of the object supported in the palm of one's hand – rather than just holding part of the object between two fingers. Finger rings should not be placed on fingers, as the metal could be brittle and can break under the pressure. Even better, handling should be avoided entirely by viewing objects

8 *Good practice: working on finds in the home. Note how our finder has a good source of light, is examining his find through a stand-alone magnifier, has ensured that his object is well supported and that he is wearing gloves. Whilst he take notes he has also ensured that his other finds have been kept sealed in their airtight polythene box.* Copyright Kate Morton

in their own crystal boxes with a 'Plastazote' foam support specially cut out in the shape of the find. This is because a find might appear to be stable and solid but due to corrosion could be a lot more fragile than it looks. Soil may be all that is holding an object together – clumsy and careless handling can easily result in damage.

Conservators usually wear gloves when handling objects – this is to protect both the object and the person. Even clean hands carry moisture, grease, acids and salts which can be left on the surface of artefacts and accelerate corrosion. An example of this are finger-marks often seen as areas of tarnish on polished silver surfaces. When these impurities are left on the corroded surfaces of archaeological metalwork, they can promote corrosion of any remaining metal parts. Hands should ALWAYS be washed before and after handling all archaeological finds.

Good practice for handling objects:

✓ Wash hands before handling objects, and ideally wear gloves (for example thin latex or nitrile gloves) to protect yourself as well as the object.

✓ After handling, hands should always be washed again; lead and copper corrosion products in particular are toxic.

✓ Minimise handling: instead use clear 'crystal' storage boxes so that the artefact can be viewed without any direct contact.

Step 2: What is it made of?

Deciding what an object is and what it is made of is crucial for ensuring that it receives the right kind of treatment. Sometimes it may be very obvious: coins and tokens are usually easily recognized, as are everyday household objects such as spoons, and personal items like buckles or finger rings. Other objects may be almost impossible to recognize: lumps of corroded iron are the most obvious example.

The type of object (coin, spoon, ring) may be obvious but what it is made of may not be. The appearance and properties of an ancient metal object when it is excavated may be very different to those of the object when it was new. Over time, with exposure to moisture and air most metals corrode, and they revert to their natural mineral forms. The corrosion of the metals of antiquity is discussed in chapter 3.

However, the appearance, especially the colour of the corrosion products, can provide clues about the type of metal or alloy from which an artefact was made. If left uncleaned, the appearance of the corrosion can also help to tell more about the objects original composition and its current condition.

The appearance of corrosion products depends not only on the nature of the metal or alloy but also on the conditions of its burial. The type of soil, how acid or alkaline the soil was, and the amount of water and oxygen in the soil, all influence corrosion. Corrosion often occurs in layers – each layer being a different colour or shade of colour. In **Table 2**, the colour of the outermost layer, even though it may be mixed with soil, is listed as the first clue to identifying the metal or alloy.

The ways in which different metals corrode and how this can determine where the 'original surface' of an object lies are discussed in more detail in chapter 3.

Step 3: Is it treasure?

If the initial assessment of the metal suggests strongly that the artefact is made of gold or silver, then the find may need to be reported as treasure. Treasure can be defined as all objects of gold or silver more than 300 years old; in the case of gold and silver coins, there need to be two or more coins from the same find to qualify. The Treasure Act also applies to groups of ten or more base metal coins found as a group, and in future will be extended to cover groups of prehistoric base metal objects. Items found in or associated with wrecks (flotsam, jetsam, derelict and

Table 2 Colour as a basic first clue
to the identification of corroded metals

COLOUR of outermost layer of corrosion	METAL OR ALLOY	OTHER CLUES
Yellow/Gold	Gold	Un-corroded bright metal Soft, easily marked
	Brass	Un-corroded dull metal
	'Fools gold' or iron pyrites	
Green	Copper and alloys of copper, e.g. bronze, brass, base silver	
Silver/Grey	Silver	May be uncorroded, bright metal
	Speculum = copper/tin alloy	Dull silver/grey colour Hard
	Lead and its alloys	Very heavy in relation to size Soft
Dark brown-orange	Iron	Attracted by magnet even if corroded
Black	Iron	Attracted by magnet
	Copper and its alloys	
	Silver and its alloys	
	Lead and its alloys	
Blue	Copper and its alloys	Not usual in UK – requires very dry burial environment (e.g. Egypt)
	Iron	Attracted by magnet

lagan found in or on the shores of the sea or any tidal water) are covered by the Merchant Shipping Act 1995, and need to be reported to the Receiver of Wreck. For more information on treasure and wreck, please see Appendix 1.

It is very important that no cleaning or reshaping of potential treasure finds is attempted. They should be kept simply as they have been found, and reported as soon as is possible to the local museum or finds liaison officer (see Appendix 3). Finders are also strongly advised in any case to seek professional help in the field if they believe they have discovered treasure (see chapter 4).

Step 4: To dry or not to dry?

Metal objects which have been in the soil for many centuries may have reached an equilibrium with their burial environment and active corrosion may almost have ceased. However, when objects are excavated they are suddenly exposed to a very different environment, and this change can cause metals to actively corrode afresh. Two factors are needed for metal to corrode: moisture and oxygen. Both of these are present in abundance in the normal atmosphere – what conservators call ambient conditions. Reducing moisture (humidity levels) and/or oxygen levels around metal objects will therefore reduce their rate of corrosion. In practical terms, it is generally easier to reduce the moisture around an object – to dry it and keep it in dry conditions – than to reduce its exposure to oxygen.

To dry

Metal objects recovered from British soils will contain some moisture when excavated and will be at least damp when found. For most metal finds, it will be good practice to allow the objects to dry once back home before packing and storing them. Exceptions to this are discussed below.

Whilst different conservators may favour different ways of drying finds, the following advice is felt by the authors to enable finds to be dried in a way that should be safe for the majority of metal finds.

Good practice

✓ Take each object out of its bag carefully, and lay it on top of its bag to dry.
✓ Dry objects at normal room temperature – this may take a few hours or a few days depending on the size of the object.
✓ If a very sensitive pair of scales is available, the drying process can be monitored by noting the weight of the object at regular intervals: when there is no more weight loss the object will be 'dry' – it will have reached equilibrium with the surrounding air.
✓ Leave waterlogged and composite objects (see below) wet and seek professional conservation advice immediately – see contacts in Appendix 3.

Bad practice

✗ Do not try and speed up the drying process – for example with a fan heater (**9**) or by putting the objects in the airing cupboard. This could lead to the object drying too quickly and cause damage such as cracking.
✗ Do not cover finds with 'Vaseline', 'WD-40' or olive oil – an object may not be as 'dry' as you think and these products can seal in moisture and cause corrosion (see also chapter 9).
✗ Do not put objects in direct sunlight or on radiators to dry – the sudden temperature fluctuations could cause stresses in the object and lead to damage, such as cracking.

9 *Bad practice: fan heaters should not be used to dry finds. Finds should be allowed to dry in their own time at room temperature.* Copyright Kate Morton

Not to dry: waterlogged and composite objects

Objects with both metal and non-metal parts (for example, an iron knife with a bone handle) are called composite objects. These will, not surprisingly, often contain components which have different storage requirements and compromises will need to be made. It is strongly recommended that such objects are looked at by a professional conservator who can advise on the best treatment and storage for that particular object. As a general rule, on excavation of such an object it is best to keep it in conditions as near as possible to those from which it has just been removed – i.e. damp or wet, dark, cool and sealed from the air as much as possible.

Metal finds with glass parts (for example enamelled objects or stained glass still attached to lead frames or cames) should also normally be kept damp. If very degraded, the glass may break up while it dries out – a small piece should be tested first and dried slowly. If it starts to break up, the drying should be stopped and advice sought.

Metal with pottery is normally safe to dry.

Good practice

✓ Do not dry metal finds with organic components – seek advice from a professional conservator first.

✓ Keep composite and waterlogged finds damp in a place which is dark, cool and sealed from the air (keeping the finds dark and cool will prevent mould growth). A household fridge is a good example of such a place, but not the freezer, as this is too cold.

✓ Do not dry metal with glass components if on test-drying the glass starts to break up – seek advice from a professional conservator.

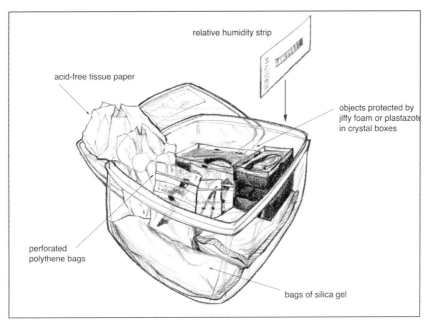

relative humidity strip

acid-free tissue paper

objects protected by
jiffy foam or plastazote
in crystal boxes

perforated
polythene bags

bags of silica gel

10 *Good practice: storing objects in the home. Finds have been placed in either individual perforated polythene bags or padded crystal boxes, and crumpled acid free tissue provides additional support and stops any movement when the box is sealed. Silica gel has been added to control moisture, and an RH indicator strip has been placed down the side to allow humidity to be monitored without the need for the lid to be removed.* Copyright Kate Morton

Step 5: Packing and storing finds

Once finds which are suitable for drying have been dried, it is good practice to pack and store objects in the correct materials and environments, as quickly as possible after excavation, to prevent damage and deterioration (**10**; **colour plate 12**). Such preventive conservation measures aim to minimise deterioration. Complete preservation cannot be guaranteed because no natural environment can entirely prevent deterioration, but every effort can be made to provide an environment that will slow it down. Conservators and conservation scientists have studied the nature and deterioration of archaeological materials and can recommend suitable environments for the storage (and display) of different materials.

It is important that untreated and uncleaned finds be stored properly (whether dry or wet) as soon as they are brought home. Packing and storing in the right materials and environment will minimise deterioration, and thus provide time for objects to be examined, recorded and treated with care, and excluding the need to rush the process. As detectorists build up their collections, they should think of them as part of the country's heritage held in their safe-keeping, and therefore in need of being properly curated and cared for.

Packing materials

Packing materials used should meet the following criteria:

- Provide the object with physical support and protection.
- Enable an appropriate storage environment to be created.
- Be chemically inert – so that they do not cause deterioration of the object.
- Reduce the need for direct handling by allowing the object to be viewed within its packing.

Table 3 lists suitable packing materials. Some of these have been discussed in chapter 4 on how to look after finds in the field. Most can be easily obtained in the local high street at very low cost. Some of the materials listed are more specialised, and a list of suppliers is given in Appendix 3. Many suppliers and manufacturers will only supply large quantities of material, but it is often cheaper to buy these products in bulk. It may be worth buying them with colleagues or through your local metal detecting club. Your local museum curator or finds liaison officer should be able to help, either by selling on small amounts of material, or recommending a good supplier (for contacts, see Appendix 3).

Table 3 lists materials which should be used, but there are a number of common materials which should be avoided: ordinary paper; tissue; cardboard; rubber-based foams; newspaper; some woods (especially oak) and wool-based materials such as felt. All these materials give off acidic vapours which will cause corrosion of metals. Some conservation suppliers sell specially treated cardboard and paper which are safe to use with metal finds. Cotton wool is another material which should not be used for packing objects – fibres get caught in corrosion and are very difficult to remove!

Packing objects

Each object should be placed either in an individual self-seal polythene bag or in an individual polystyrene ('crystal') box. If using a polythene bag it should be pierced with numerous small holes (**2**) before the object is put inside.

Some padding or support for an object in a bag can be provided by cutting a thin piece of polythene ('jiffy') foam or 'Plastazote' to fit inside the bag with the object (**colour plate 13**). Objects put into 'crystal' boxes will need some padding for support and to stop them rattling about. Such support can be provided either by crumpled acid-free tissue – to provide a nest for the object – or by using 'Plastazote' (polythene foam) (**colour plate 12**). If using 'Plastazote', a hollow in the shape of the object can be cut into it to provide a protective recess for the object (**colour plate 21**). Further padding should be placed in the lid of the box. Packing objects may seem to be an easy thing but it takes care and thought to ensure that the object is softly and securely held in position without being squashed and crushed.

Table 3   Suitable packing materials for objects

Plastic boxes (polythene or polypropylene)	With self-seal (snap on) lids, such as freezer storage boxes e.g. 'Tupperware'
Polythene bags	Self sealing if possible. Make numerous small holes near the top so that air can circulate. The bag should be a suitable size for the object
Polystyrene boxes ('crystal' boxes)	Clear rigid plastic with hinged or detachable lids
Polythene foam (non absorbent)	e.g. 'Jiffy' foam, or 'Plastazote'. The latter may have recesses cut to fit the object
Polyether foam (water absorbent)	Foam with open cell structure
'Bubble wrap'	Used to cushion finds stored in larger boxes. Should never be in direct contact with objects: the smooth side should be nearest to the packing material for the object(s). This is because the bubbles can sometimes mark soft objects and may trap moisture at an object's surface
Acid free tissue paper	Used crumpled, to provide a bed or pillow for objects, e.g. within a crystal box. A smooth piece of tissue should be placed between the crumpled paper pillow and the object – especially if the latter is silver or gold which could be easily scratched
Polythene labels	e.g. 'Tyvek' (will not deteriorate even in the dampest storage environments)
Black ballpoint pens	Used to mark bags and labels. They will leave an imprint that is a useful backup if the ink fades or is rubbed off
Permanent black felt tip pens	Used to mark plastic boxes, bags and labels (do not use these to mark the actual objects) e.g. 'Artline' pens
Silica gel	Used to create a dry storage environment
Relative humidity indicator strips	Placed inside polythene boxes to indicate and monitor dryness or dampness of micro-environment. They should be placed in a position where they are visible through the side of the box

The bags or boxes containing the finds should then be placed together inside an airtight plastic box. If the finds are to be kept dry a sachet or polythene bag (pierced with numerous small holes) containing silica gel should be placed in the bottom of the box (see below). Any empty space in the outer box can be packed with crumpled acid-free tissue, 'jiffy' foam or bubble wrap to prevent objects rattling about and being damaged when moved (**10**). If the finds in the outer box are to be kept waterlogged or in a damp condition then wet absorbent polyether foam can be used in the outer box instead of silica gel and dry packing materials.

Creating the right environment for finds

Moisture and air (oxygen) can cause metals to corrode. Thus removing moisture and consequently keeping metals dry can prevent corrosion. In the long term, all metals can benefit from being dried and stored in a dry environment.

The more unstable the metal, the drier its storage environment needs to be. Thus conservators usually recommend that iron needs to be kept in a much drier environment than gold (see also chapter 3).

Relative humidity (RH)

Moisture in the air is normally measured as a percentage of the total amount of moisture the air can hold, and this is dependent on temperature: at high temperature, air is able to hold more water. (Anyone who has ever visited a tropical country will know that the air is often very hot and sticky because it contains a high level of moisture.) The term used to describe the amount of moisture in the air is relative humidity (RH for short). 100% relative humidity is very wet and 0% relative humidity is very dry.

Most metal objects, unless they need to be kept wet in the short term as discussed in Step 4, above, are best kept in a dry or desiccated environment. **Table 4** provides a summary of the different types of storage environment which should be used for different types of metal and composite objects.

Silica gel and health and safety

Silica gel can be used to create a dry environment within a sealed container. It does this by absorbing water from the atmosphere in which it is placed. This is why new cameras when they are sold will invariably have a small sachet of silica gel in their box, to help prevent moisture getting into the lens.

Some silica gel is self indicating – its colour changes with the amount of moisture it contains. Until recently most conservators used a blue self-indicating silica gel, which was pink when wet and dark blue when dry (below approximately 40%). However, the blue colour is due to the addition of cobalt chloride which has been found to present a health hazard, particularly if the gel is purchased as loose granules – and there is also a dust hazard.

Table 4: Storage environments for different materials

Material	Storage environment	Notes
Metals: iron and actively corroding copper alloys	**very dry** (i.e. desiccated) with silica gel Iron less than 20% RH Copper alloy less than 35% RH Temperature 16-25°C	Suitable for short and long term storage
Metals: gold, silver, lead, pewter, stable copper alloys	**dry** normal (ambient) conditions, in a dry place in the house – but preferably in a box with some silica gel 40-60% RH 16-25°C	Suitable for short and long term storage. The airing cupboard is not a good dry place – it is too hot
Metals with substantial (non-mineralised) organic wood, leather, textiles, bone, ivory) which remain attached	**damp** (not wet), **cool** (refrigerated, but not frozen) and **dark** i.e. keep in conditions as close to the burial environment as possible 90-100% RH *c.*5°C	Short term storage ONLY – advice from a professional conservator should be sought as soon as possible
Metals with glassy components such as enamel		
Metal with painted stone, and plaster		
Metal with amber, jet and shale		
All materials from underwater marine sites	**wet, cool, dark** (refrigerated but not frozen) 100% RH	Short term storage ONLY – advice from a professional conservator should be sought as soon as possible
Metals with organic components (e.g. wood, leather, textiles) from waterlogged burial environments		

Suppliers of silica gel (see Appendix 3) are now selling safer types, and the loose self-indicating blue gel is being replaced in museums. We would recommend that silica gel that is already sealed into porous bags be purchased, rather than loose gel. Sachets which have been stitched are preferable to heat-sealed ones, as the latter may come apart when reactivating (see below). If loose gel is used, then it should be placed in its own perforated polythene bags before being put into the outer plastic box with the objects, and a dust mask and gloves should be worn when transferring gel between containers. Loose silica gel should never be in direct contact with objects as it can cause abrasion.

One final point is that although getting hold of silica gel might be rather laborious, it can be reused (see below). Also members of metal detecting clubs might consider buying a bulk supply for distribution to club members.

How much silica gel to use

To create a dry environment for metal objects in a sealed container use about 100g of dry silica gel per litre of box space. In imperial measurements, that is about 2oz per pint. A 10 litre storage box should contain about 1kg of dry silica gel, while a 1 gallon box should contain about 1lb of dry silica gel.

Making sure the environment is dry

Once all the objects are in individual bags or boxes, packing materials and silica gel are inside the main storage box and the lid firmly replaced to seal the box, it is then important to be able to monitor the RH inside it. The best way to do this is to use a relative humidity indicating strip.

If the plastic box is clear enough, the RH indicating strip can be taped to the inside of the box so that the strip, which changes colour according to RH, can be seen from the outside – without needing to open the box. **Table 4** gives guidance on what RH level the strip should show for different types of storage environment.

RH indicator strips can be purchased from the suppliers given in Appendix 3.

Making silica gel last

Silica gel will need to be dried out (or reactivated) when it can no longer maintain the desired RH within the sealed container. The frequency with which this is required will depend on the seal on the box, the number of times the box is opened, the quantity of gel used and on the amount of moisture in the objects and packing materials when first put into the box. When finds are recently excavated, the silica gel may need to be changed or dried out several times before a very dry environment is created and maintained.

How to dry silica gel

If the silica gel is in the manufacturer's ready-made cloth bags, these can be placed on a baking tray in an oven at 100-120°C. The oven should be clear of any fat or grease since these could coat the gel and prevent it from working. The oven door may need to be opened occasionally during the drying process to allow moisture to escape.

The drying time needed will depend on the amount of moisture absorbed by the silica gel. If self-indicating gel in bags is used, a colour change from pink to dark blue will indicate that it is dry (but please see the health and safety advice above).

If non self-indicating gel is being dried, progress could be monitored by weighing the bags every half hour on a good pair of kitchen scales. When no further weight change is recorded, the gel can be assumed to be dry again.

Loose self-indicating silica gel can be dried in the same way as for bags, as described above. The loose gel needs to be thinly spread (no thicker than half an inch) on the baking tray.

Silica gel can be reused indefinitely as long as it is not overheated when being reactivated. If it goes brown it should be discarded and replaced with new gel.

Table 5   Spotting signs of trouble – indicators of active corrosion

Metal	Signs of trouble – active corrosion
IRON	Appearance of orange liquid drops on surface (**colour plate 14**)
	Appearance of bright orange powdery corrosion (**colour plate 15**)
	Object starts to flake, laminate and crack (**colour plate 15**)
LEAD/TIN ALLOYS	Appearance of white powdery corrosion (**colour plate 16**)
COPPER ALLOYS	Appearance of very pale green, powdery spots or patches – 'bronze disease' (**colour plates 17 & 18**)
SILVER	White/grey corrosion may turn lilac – this is a change in the mineral (silver chloride) but does not indicate active corrosion of underlying metal. Alloyed metals, with copper, may exhibit green corrosion as above
GOLD	Unlikely to be any change on excavation. Alloyed metals may corrode as above

Step 6: Spotting signs of trouble

Once finds have been correctly stored in the home, they will need to be monitored to ensure that they are not starting to corrode. **Table 5** lists some visual indicators that a metal object is actively corroding. If any of these are spotted, or if there is any change in the general appearance of an object, it is likely to indicate that the storage environment is not dry enough to prevent corrosion. The silica gel may need to be changed, or dried out, or more silica gel may be needed to create a drier environment. If the object continues to corrode, then advice should be sought from a professional conservator.

If any of these problems are encountered, finders are advised to seek the help of a professional conservator (see Appendix 3), and also to refer to chapters 7 and 9. Even if objects are actively corroding, they should still be kept in good storage conditions to keep the progress of the corrosion to a minimum, so the advice on storage provided above should still be adhered to.

Summary

This chapter has provided advice on good practice for handling and storing objects in the home, how to decide what metals finds consist of and whether or not they should be dried, whether finds need to be declared treasure, and how to spot signs of trouble. The next chapter looks at how finds can be more closely examined and recorded.

6 Examining and recording finds

In the last chapter, advice was provided on how objects can be stored to help prevent further deterioration. In this chapter and the next, guidance will be provided on how objects can be handled and examined and which interventive conservation techniques might be used by conservators to improve their appearance and find out more about them.

Examining artefacts

Examination is a vital first stage of any conservation work in order to determine the nature and condition of an object. All finds are thoroughly examined by a conservator before they begin cleaning or any other treatment. Any information about condition, visible features and the texture and colour of corrosion products is recorded before attempting to remove soil and corrosion products from the artefact.

Examination can lead to the discovery of evidence about what an object is, how it might have been used and how it was made. It can also reveal information about the nature and condition of the object that can help in its care and treatment.

The most common method of examination used by conservators is visual inspection – simply looking at an object can reveal a great deal. This is usually done with the aid of a microscope and x-radiography. When information on the composition or metallurgical structure is needed, more sophisticated techniques are used. Whenever possible, non-destructive techniques (i.e. where no samples are removed) are employed.

Visual inspection

Many interesting and important details can be discovered using a stereo (binocular) microscope (10 to 40 times magnification), and this is the main way in which professional conservators will examine objects (**colour plate 23**). A basic binocular microscope can now be acquired from as little as £300 new, and second-hand microscopes can be even cheaper. If individual members are not able to purchase a microscope for themselves, their metal detector club might consider buying one for use by its members. Alternatively, another option for home use would be a good magnifying glass, which is not particularly expensive. The best types are those which are on an adjustable stand, because these will allow both hands to be used to examine artefacts. These should be used in conjunction with a bright light (**8**).

X-rays

X-radiography, or x-raying for short, is something which the vast majority of people are familiar with, as it is a routine part of dental check-ups and operations in hospital. It might come as a surprise to some readers, however, that conservators also use x-ray machines to examine metal objects. The advantage of x-rays is that they can be used to gain information about an object without having to carry out any cleaning.

The extent to which x-rays pass through an artefact depends on its thickness, density and the type of material from which it is made. The artefact is placed in a shielded enclosure and bombarded with x-rays. The image is recorded on x-radiographic film or displayed on a screen. Details of form and construction can be seen, as well as the presence of other metals, platings, inlays and components. An x-radiographic image can also indicate the extent of an object's corrosion. The use of x-radiography is a routine part of the archaeological process for all iron objects and many other metal artefacts, particularly copper alloys.

X-radiography is especially important for iron artefacts, because corrosion can be so disfiguring that it can be extremely difficult to work out what the object actually is. An Anglo-Saxon iron buckle from Buckland cemetery, Kent, provides a very good example. As found (**colour plate 19**), the object looked like a fairly uninteresting lump of iron corrosion. X-raying, however, revealed not only the shape of the buckle, but beautiful and sophisticated copper alloy and silver inlay on both the plate and the frame, all before any cleaning had begun (**colour plate 20**). The conservator was then able to use the x-radiograph to help guide the cleaning of the object (**colour plate 21**). For this reason, professional conservators will always take an x-ray of an iron object as part of the examination process.

Interpretation of the x-ray takes into account the extent of corrosion, type of artefact, and the x-ray exposure time involved. An object may also be x-rayed from several angles to provide three-dimensional information. The 'original surface' of the object can often be seen on the x-radiograph, preserved as a denser layer within the corrosion. The advantage of this for conservators is that they then have a guide to cleaning. Cleaning an object without an x-radiograph is working 'blind', and the chances of damaging the object can thus be greatly increased.

X-radiography is not as widely used by professional conservators when they examine lead and tin alloy items. This is partly due to the density of lead preventing x-rays passing through the object, x-radiography also being unnecessary when the corrosion can preserve the original shape so well. It can be of use when looking at objects such as thin seals, pendants and pilgrim badges. In such instances, technological evidence such as casting flaws and seam lines can be revealed as well as evidence of the object's form and condition.

Getting finds X-rayed

X-ray machines are extremely expensive, which means that finders or clubs are extremely unlikely to be able to afford an actual machine of their own. But having x-rays made of iron objects in particular is not impossible, and becomes cheaper the more objects which are examined, as a number of finds (depending on their size) can be x-rayed on one plate. So readers are advised that if they have iron objects which they want to have x-rayed, they should contact their local finds liaison officer, museum curator or conservator to see if x-rays can be made on their behalf. Metal detector groups might also be able to club together to have some of their iron artefacts x-rayed. A list of contacts is provided in Appendix 3.

Analytical techniques

Various analytical techniques are sometimes used to discover more about an artefact. They can provide information on dating, manufacture and even the origin of the metal. Some techniques, such as Scanning Electron Microscopy (SEM), can tell us about the composition of a metal artefact or its corrosion products, whilst other forms of analysis, such as Fourier Transform, Infrared Spectroscopy (FT-IR), may be used to reveal more about organic remains preserved in the corrosion products. If finders wish to know more about these, they would be advised to contact a professional conservator, or an archaeological scientist, since these techniques cannot be done without highly specialised equipment.

What examination can reveal

The above methods are used by conservators to examine finds, and can reveal important information, ranging from how the object was constructed to the remains of any organic material in which the object was buried.

Evidence of burial or use

Certain minerals (corrosion products) can provide clues about the kind of environment in which an object has been buried and even of changes in that environment over time. For example, on an iron artefact, black, grey or occasionally golden sulphide deposits on the surface usually indicate that an object has been buried in an oxygen-free waterlogged environment. The blue iron phosphate (vivianite) is found on objects recovered from organic-rich and phosphate-rich environments such as cess-pits. The brick-red iron oxide haematite may indicate that an object was burnt prior to burial or during the burial process, as it is usually only found on iron objects heated to above 200-300°C.

Evidence of other metals

Evidence of metal coatings, decoration and solders may only be preserved as fragile corrosion products. A grey/lilac silver chloride layer, for example, may be all that remains of a once silvered metal surface. A deposit inside a crevice could indicate the location of a soldered join. As metals have different potentials to corrode, some metals may be preserved by the preferential corrosion of another less stable metal which is in direct contact with the object. An example of this would be a well-preserved copper alloy buckle with its iron pin missing because it had completely corroded away.

The colour and composition of any excavated metal object can be very different to its original state because of the leaching out of other metals from the alloy during burial. For example, brass may appear pinker than its original colour because of the loss of zinc.

Evidence of inorganic materials (e.g. enamel)

Metal artefacts were sometimes decorated or inlaid with enamel or mounted with semi-precious stones (**colour plate 22**). Gemstones are mostly stable and will often appear unaffected when excavated. Glass or enamel, however, can deteriorate during burial and become stained by corrosion products. The appearance of degraded enamels can also be very similar to that of copper-alloy corrosion products, because copper salts were used to produce the colour of the enamel. Careful examination of a Roman brooch, for example, can reveal remains that resemble brown sugar in recessed areas. This can be all that is left to indicate the presence of a glass or enamel inlay. Cast metal artefacts, if broken or damaged, can reveal remnants of a clay casting core which indicate how the artefact was made.

Evidence of organic materials preserved in corrosion products

Many metal objects were originally made and/or used in conjunction with organic materials such as wood, antler or ivory for handles, and leather for belt straps or scabbards (**colour plates 5-8**). Metal objects may have been in close contact with organic materials, such as a copper alloy brooch used to pin clothing, or they could be stored in wooden, leather or cloth containers. Traces of these more perishable organic materials sometimes survive on or around the objects, for example in sockets or on tangs. They are frequently preserved or replaced by the corrosion minerals and can be seen as impressions or casts of the organic material. In this form they are often referred to by conservators as 'mineral preserved organics'.

Organic material often survives intact in waterlogged environments, where air is excluded. In certain burial environments, corrosion, especially on copper alloy artefacts, may preserve traces of organic materials. The toxic nature of copper corrosion often inhibits bacteria and mould growth. This means that organic components of metal objects may also be preserved in damp conditions even where air is plentiful.

Recording information about objects

Documentation is one of the most important aspects of a conservator's job, and there is no reason why metal detectorists should not also keep records of their finds. A detectorist may tap his or her head and say 'I can tell you exactly where I found this brooch, what it is made of and how I have looked after it', which is all well and good, but when the detectorist is no longer with us, no one else will know this information unless it has been written down.

Detectorists should keep records of where and when they have found objects, what the objects are and when they date to, and any relevant reference material for the find (for example, a reference to North's *English Hammered Coins*). From a conservation point of view, records should also be kept about any treatments or cleaning which has been applied. If the object should then need further treatment in the future, by someone else, this will be much more effective if they can know what was done to it before. For example, if a lacquer had been applied to a piece, knowing what that lacquer was would be enormously helpful if someone in the future wished to remove it.

Conservation records

Conservators will carefully keep records such as photographs and x-rays, and records of what they have seen on objects under examination. Conservation treatments are also recorded. This is because a treatment may change the nature of the artefact; for instance, chemicals or adhesives may be introduced to an artefact, or abrasive cleaning may have been used to remove part of the corrosion. Well-kept records will help to avoid confusion over the original composition or construction of an artefact. If a treatment needs to be reversed, it is essential to know what materials were originally used during conservation.

Some treatments can leave residues that may also be hazardous for those handling or working on the objects in the future. The best example of this is the application of benzotriazole (BTA), which is known to be popular with detectorists, and is discussed more fully in chapter 9. Information about these chemicals can help to avoid exposure particularly if future investigative cleaning takes place.

To summarise, conservation records may include:

- Numbers that identify the object individually.
- A line drawing of the artefact, photographs before and after treatment and x-rays.
- A description of the artefact and an accurate record of where and when it was found.
- Details of the object's condition, noting any signs of active deterioration.
- Details discovered on examination such as: nature of corrosion, traces of associated material, aspects of the object's structure and technology and the object's decoration.
- Any changes in the object's appearance since excavation.
- Results of any analytical work.
- Details of treatments undertaken including: methods used, the exact nature of any products used, observations on the effect of the treatment.
- Post-treatment condition.
- Storage methods and advice for long-term care.

Summary

This chapter has looked at the ways in which objects can be examined to reveal more information about them, the sorts of information which can be revealed, and how this information should be documented. The next chapter looks at interventive conservation techniques professional conservators may use if they wish to clean finds.

7 Cleaning objects: professional approaches

This chapter looks at some of the investigative conservation cleaning techniques which might be used by professional conservators to reveal and understand more about archaeological metal objects.

What this chapter does **not** do is provide a step-by-step guide on how to clean finds. This is impossible to do because every object is different, which means that there is no simple set of instructions which can be listed for detectorists to follow and apply to objects as in a recipe book. However, we hope that this chapter will provide some idea of the possibilities and of the factors which conservators take into account when deciding how to treat an object.

The next chapter looks at some popular cleaning methods which we advise should be avoided. At the end of the day, objects which are in private hands are the responsibility of their owner and it is up to them to decide how to treat or not to treat an object. As professionals we are not in a position to dictate how artefacts should be treated; we can only advise. However, we do ask that three very important points are considered before any cleaning is attempted by metal detectorists:

1. Think about whether or not it is really necessary to clean an object to understand more about it.

2. Once an object has been cleaned, remember that it is not possible to put back what has been removed.

3. Think about risks: could cleaning damage the object, and thereby reduce its value, both historically and financially?

Conservation cleaning requires a thorough knowledge and understanding of metal artefacts, the ways in which they have been made and the nature and appearance of corrosion – as well as knowledge and understanding of cleaning methods and the skill to apply them. Cleaning is also a deceptively simple term for what can prove to be an extremely controversial activity as it contradicts a fundamental principle of conservation practice: that conservation treatments should be reversible.

In a museum, reasons for cleaning objects may be as basic as to just keep them looking attractive to visitors and easily understood. Keeping objects free of dust and airborne dirt in the museum environment is also good preventive conservation because air borne pollutants can promote corrosion. Cleaning, however, can also be an essential part of the archaeological process to reveal more information about an object.

Investigative conservation

Investigative conservation is the term used, in relation to archaeological metal objects, to describe the removal of soil and obscuring corrosion products to uncover information about the object. It is undertaken as part of the archaeological process and is an essential part of recovering evidence. The original form, surfaces and construction of an object can be revealed through investigative conservation.

What and how much to remove
Cleaning involves removing something, irreversibly, but what and how much? Things that could be removed include burial soil, corrosion and corrosion promoters. If cleaning is done without appropriate knowledge and skill, it can easily remove 'original surfaces', as well as corrosion layers that provide protection against further corrosion, and/or organic material preserved within corrosion products. Inappropriate cleaning can also destroy evidence of manufacture, use and where the object came from (its provenance).

Corroded metals will be in a weakened state and do not have the properties of the original metal. Care must therefore be taken to avoid putting pressure on a degraded artefact. Excavated silver in particular may be brittle, due to corrosion within the metal microstructure. Objects made from sheet metal (for example vessels) are likely to be much more fragile, brittle and corroded than solid cast objects.

To determine how far to go when cleaning metal objects, the conservator needs a comprehensive understanding of corrosion processes. The extent to which metal objects corrode depends on many factors, but the appearance of an excavated object is likely to be very different from that when it was originally in use. The location of the 'original surface' depends on the nature of the metal and the burial environment.

An x-radiograph (see chapter 6) is often used as a guide to cleaning and may help to reveal evidence of features such as surface decoration which can then be revealed by careful investigative cleaning. An x-radiograph is always produced before any cleaning is carried out on iron artefacts.

Throughout any cleaning process, objects are continually examined for emerging evidence of different corrosion products and for traces of plating, inlays and enamels, and of preserved wood, leather and textile. Anything found is then carefully recorded and cleaning halted before the evidence is destroyed.

The extent and manner of investigative conservation cleaning should be determined by the following factors:

- the physical condition of the object.
- its likely composition (e.g. percentage of copper in a base silver).
- the extent of the corrosion.
- facilities available.
- the skill, expertise and knowledge of the person undertaking the cleaning.

'Original surface'

If further information is required about an object, a conservator will normally remove corrosion down to a level that preserves the detail of the 'original surface' of the artefact. This 'original surface' does not necessarily lie at the surface of the surviving metal; rather, the best detail is most often preserved within the corrosion layers. It may be extremely difficult to recognise the often subtle changes within the corrosion which indicate the location of the 'original surface'. The overlying layers of corrosion may also be considerably harder than the levels of corrosion which indicate the original shape and detail of an object's surface. Thus indiscriminate cleaning of such artefacts could completely remove/destroy their 'original surface'. See also chapter 3 for discussion of original surfaces on the different metals of antiquity.

Methods of cleaning used by professional conservators

Investigative cleaning techniques can be broadly described as manual, mechanical or chemical. A conservator may use a combination of all three on an object. Generally, cleaning will always start with the mildest, least interventive, method.

The condition of the surface must be assessed before deciding which technique will cause the least risk of damage. All methods of cleaning have the potential to cause damage if applied without appropriate knowledge, skill and understanding of both the object and the cleaning method.

Manual cleaning

Manual cleaning involves using small hand tools such as scalpels, scrapers (wood and metal) and a range of soft brushes, for example, artist's paint brushes, to remove corrosion or hard surface concretions. Work is normally done under magnification of around x10 to x40, and often with the aid of an x-ray. If such cleaning is attempted in the home, a good magnifying glass on a stand with a bright light should be used if a microscope is not available (**8**). This method is preferred by most professional conservators for removing the soil and loose corrosion and for reducing harder corrosion crusts.

All the tools mentioned above can be easily purchased (**colour plate 24**). Sharp blades can be bought from stationery or artist shops. Wooden tools are often made by conservators themselves, for example from cocktail sticks. Soft metals such as lead, silver and gold can be easily scratched by metal tools so softer tools such as brushes or a wooden stick, shaped to a point or chisel-like tip, are preferred. Soft brushes can be easily obtained from DIY or artist's shops. Always remember that some of these tools are dangerous, and should be used with great care and never left lying around in the home.

Some conservators also use glass bristle brushes. These should only be used if a binocular microscope is available to view the object as it is cleaned, as they can very easily leave fine scratch marks on the original surface (**colour plate 25**). Broken bristles can also be left on the surface which are only visible under magnification. When using glass bristle brushes, conservators always wear gloves to prevent bristles getting stuck in their skin. These brushes can be purchased from specialist conservation suppliers (see Appendix 3).

If any of the manual cleaning methods described are attempted in the home, the following health warnings **must** be followed:

- Scalpel blades must be carefully removed and disposed of in a way to prevent injury. For example used blades can be wrapped in tissue paper and bound up with sticky tape.
- Protective gloves should be worn when cleaning all metals. This is because corrosion products can be very harmful, and also because any tools used might also be dangerous – particularly glass bristle brushes. Eye protection should also be worn.
- A mask should be worn when cleaning all metals but particularly lead. This is because the corrosion dust produced when cleaning metals (particularly lead dust) is a health hazard.

Mechanical cleaning using machines

Where corrosion is particularly hard, the use of powered tools is sometimes more appropriate and effective than hand tools. Some of the mechanical cleaning tools used by conservators are described here. Mechanical tools must be used in a controlled manner to ensure that no harm is done to the object.

Machines and tools using compressed air

Conservators use two specialised items of equipment which use compressed air: air-abrasive machines and pneumatic pens. An air-abrasive machine works by carrying a very fine abrasive powder to the surface of the object in a jet of compressed air from a hand-held nozzle with a small opening. The air pressure, and the type and quantity of powder can all be varied to provide a flexible, sensitive cleaning tool. Used with skill and knowledge an air-abrasive machine can sometimes clean more gently than hand tools, but it can also do far more damage, more quickly, if inappropriately or inexpertly used. It is particularly used by conservators to reveal the shape and surface detail of corroded iron artefacts.

A pneumatic pen also uses compressed air (**colour plate 26**). The vibrating stylus tip of the pen is placed against hard concretions on the object to remove them, with no pressure being exerted on the artefact. Pneumatic pens can be useful for removing corrosion from copper alloys and iron.

Compressed air tools can be dangerous and require appropriate health and safety precautions to be taken.

Electronic engraving pens

Some conservators use electronic, vibrating, engraving pens, fitted with an inter-changeable needle at the end, to remove hard corrosion products. These can be bought from specialist suppliers and may be available from some craft shops. However, there are two dangers inherent in their use. One is that the vibration which causes the corrosion to come away is also transmitted into the whole object, which can cause it to break, particularly if there are hairline cracks or fractures through it. Such cracks may be invisible to the operator. Also, prolonged use of this tool can cause a type of nerve damage to the operator, sometimes referred to as 'white finger'.

Rotary tools

Small rotary tools such as mini-drills can be fitted with a variety of polishing and grinding wheels. These can be used to remove very hard large corrosion lumps but are difficult to control and do not discriminate the more detailed surface features. If used at all, conservators tend to use such tools only on the outer layers of corrosion concretions on iron artefacts which are of historic, rather than of prehistoric, date.

Wet cleaning and the use of solvents

Water, although it can cause metals to corrode, can be an effective cleaning agent if used properly. Conservators use distilled or deionised water for wet cleaning. Tap water is not used because it contains substances such as salt (sodium chloride) which, even in minute traces, is very bad for objects because it accelerates the corrosion process. **Finders are therefore advised not to use tap water.**

Objects should never be held under a running tap (**7**) to clean them even though many detectorists are tempted to use this method to rapidly remove soil from around finds. If water is used as a cleaning agent it is best used locally, applied to the surface of the object only, rather than wetting the whole object by immersing it. Conservators use cotton wool swabs, dampened with distilled or deionised water, rolled, rather than scrubbed, across the surface of the object. This is often sufficient to lift off loose dirt or to soften harder soil sufficiently to allow manual cleaning. This method will also minimise the risk of scratching or distorting a soft or embrittled artefact, and is often all that is required to clean uncorroded metals such as gold or silver. Cleaning a lead object this way can also minimise the health risks associated with airborne lead corrosion dust.

After wet cleaning, it is vital that objects are thoroughly and quickly dried. This can be done using a hand-held dryer on a cool setting or by dehydration with a solvent such as acetone or industrial methylated spirit (IMS). Solvent drying can be done by immersing the object if it is sufficiently robust, or by applying the solvent on cotton swabs to the wet area if not. Volatile solvents, such as acetone or industrial methylated spirit (ethanol), will evaporate from the surface of an object quickly and do not affect corrosion. If they are pure, they will not leave a residue. They can also be used on a swab to remove soil from an object's surface (**colour plate 27**). Acetone is available from specialist conservation suppliers as well as from chemists. However, a customs and excise licence is needed to buy industrial methylated spirit. The purple coloured methylated spirit, which can be bought in shops, should never be used on objects as this contains piridine, which will leave harmful residues on the object.

If any solvents are used, important health and safety guidelines need to be followed:

- Acetone and IMS are flammable, so great care should be taken if used.
- Breathing in the fumes from these solvents can be harmful, so only small quantities should be used and only in well ventilated areas. Bottles and containers should also be kept covered at all times.

Chemical cleaning methods

Stripping, or the total removal of corrosion products by chemicals, was routinely practised in the past but too often this resulted in pitted metal objects that bore little resemblance to their original shapes. Now conservators prefer to use manual methods (see above) to expose the 'original surface' of metal finds.

If chemicals are used at all, conservators normally restrict their application to discrete, localised areas on an object where the process can be strictly controlled and monitored under magnification. An example where this might happen is to soften corrosion concretions or deposits from the burial environment before their removal by manual cleaning. This can be particularly helpful where the corrosion products are harder than the underlying original surface. All chemical residues must be completely removed from the object as they could continue to act on or even promote further corrosion if left. This is done by thoroughly rinsing the treated area with distilled water, on swabs, to remove chemicals. The object is then thoroughly and quickly dried.

Chemical immersion treatments (where the object is completely immersed in the solution) are rarely used because they are very difficult to control. They do not discriminate between the 'original surface' and the surrounding corrosion when the original surface is preserved within the corrosion and not at the metal surface.

The type of chemical used has to be appropriate for the type of corrosion or concretion to be removed and for the type of metal. Chemical cleaning tends to be used only on copper alloy or silver objects if there is no alternative. For example, a very dilute organic acid (5-10% in distilled water), such as formic or citric acid, may be applied very locally, on cotton swabs, to soften green carbonate corrosion, on copper alloy or base silver objects, if it is too hard to be safely removed by manual cleaning alone. Organic acids, such as formic or citric acid, are preferred to mineral acids, such as hydrochloric or sulphuric acids. The organic acids are less aggressive and tend to evaporate, thus lessening the risk of leaving damaging residues on the object's surface.

Health and Safety warning

Chemicals and corrosion products may come under the COSHH (Control of Substances Hazardous to Health) regulations, 1988. Suppliers of treatment chemicals are legally required to provide safety data sheets, which outline the nature of the substance and any hazard to health. If you are tempted to use chemicals, read the information provided carefully and follow the recommendations on safe practice, and ask for this information if it is not provided.

Summary

In this chapter, the various methods which professional conservators might use to clean objects have been discussed. In general terms, conservators will use manual and mechanical cleaning methods in preference to using solvents or chemicals. If solvents or chemicals are used, they are usually only applied to small areas of objects.

If detectorists are tempted to try any of the methods described above in the home, the following advice on good practice should be followed:

Good practice

✓ Always wear gloves when handling objects and chemicals. The only exception to this is when using any rotary tools, as the gloves can get caught up in the tool which could be dangerous.

✓ Always wash hands before and after contact with objects.

✓ Keep working surfaces clean and clear of clutter.

✓ Always ensure that objects and chemicals are kept well out of the reach of children.

✓ A dust mask should be worn when carrying out work that creates dust, because corrosion products can be very harmful if breathed in.

✓ Eye protection should be worn when working with scalpels or other tools.

✓ Chemicals must only be used in well ventilated areas, and we would strongly urge that chemicals are not used at all if possible.

✓ Food, drink or tobacco should never be consumed in the area in which work is being carried out.

✓ Archaeological objects should never be kept anywhere near food preparation areas.

✓ Chemicals or solvents should never be used anywhere near a naked flame or source of a spark.

✓ Record what has been done to the object (see chapter 6).

This chapter has looked at some of the main methods of interventive conservation treatments which professional conservators use to understand more about objects. In the next chapter, inappropriate methods for cleaning finds which are known to be used by metal detectorists are discussed.

8 Popular cleaning methods to avoid

Many metal detectorists have developed their own techniques to clean finds. Although these cleaning methods may seem to get good results, they can potentially do more harm than good, and in the longer term can greatly decrease the value of objects both historically and financially.

As a general rule, detectorists are advised to be very sceptical about techniques recommended by non-professionals, for example at metal detector club meetings or on internet sites, even if those recommending them say that their objects have 'come up very nicely' as a result. Even if these objects do look attractive, there is no way of knowing the long-term effects of the treatment used. In addition, information may have been lost in the process and the find damaged. This is particularly true of quick-fix chemical treatments, some of which are offered in the metal detecting press. Although some of these include chemicals currently used by conservators, they also include chemical treatments such as 'Calgon' (SHMP), sodium sequicarbonate (SSC) and ethylenediamine tetra-acetic acid (EDTA), no longer generally used by professional conservators.

If finders therefore wish to clean their objects, they are strongly urged to follow the guidance provided in the last chapter, or seek the advice of a professional. Conservators are also happy to speak to metal detecting groups, and if there is a finds liaison officer in the local area, they will be able to arrange this. A list of contacts can be found in Appendix 3.

✗ Washing finds under a tap

Washing finds under a tap is a common practice amongst metal detectorists (**7**). There are a number of reasons why running water over finds is not recommended:

- tap water contains substances which could be harmful to finds, for example salts.
- fast running water can be very damaging to fragile objects, as loose parts of objects could be washed away alongside soil and corrosion.
- there is no way of knowing what is being washed away, with any traces of organic material preserved within the corrosion layers almost certain to be lost.
- if objects have been dried, then washing them under a tap is a particularly harsh process which will cause a sudden and potentially damaging change in the object's environment.

The only type of object which might not suffer from being cleaned in this way (with gently running water and a soft brush) are good quality, well-preserved, gold and silver coins. (Finders are reminded that groups of one or more gold or silver coins may need to be declared as treasure: see Appendix 1). The coins should be carefully supported in one hand and there should at least be a net or gauze across the plug hole to prevent loss of fragments should any break off. With other types of object, if water is to be used at all as a cleaning agent, the guidelines given in chapter 7 should be followed, as these techniques are far less likely to damage finds. Iron finds should NEVER be cleaned with water.

✗ Cleaning using harsh brushes

Manual cleaning is a very common technique used by professional conservators, but only very gentle and controllable methods are employed (see chapter 7). When it comes to brushing finds, only soft brushes are used, and even these are used very carefully. This is because anything harsher could inadvertently remove valuable surface detail and expose the underlying metal to fresh corrosion. Using hard bristle or wire brushes is thus not recommended. Such hard brushes are likely to scratch surfaces and will allow oxygen (a corrosion agent) deeper into the layers. Tiny fragments of metal from wire brushes may also be deposited on the surface of an object and if left could activate further corrosion. Even glass bristle brushes, sometimes used by conservators, can be harmful to objects if not used correctly (**colour plate 25**).

✗ Vinegar, lemon juice, ketchup, brown sauce and cola

All these substances (**11**) affect corrosion and metals because they are acidic, although not all the acids are the same. Vinegar is mostly acetic acid, whilst lemon juice is citric acid. Cola and brown sauce both contain phosphoric acid. Each substance has the capacity to quickly strip a metal object immersed in it of its corrosion products. They may produce an object which apparently looks more like the 'original form' and seems to be pleasing to the eye, but there are a number of inherent dangers in their use.

The substances listed above should be avoided for the following reasons:

- Each acid will attack certain components of an alloy at a greater rate than others and may 'leach' out some alloy component preferentially into the solution, leaving an object with a severely weakened and porous structure. Also, because some of the constituent metals forming the original alloy have been leached out into the cleaning solution, this could mislead future analysis as to the original composition of the metal.

11 *Bad practice: harmful substances for metal finds. Foodstuffs and oils are not good for either cleaning finds or trying to stop them corroding. There are far better ways of looking after finds.* Copyright Kate Morton

- When immersing an object in these products it will absorb the liquid. However carefully the artefact is rinsed afterwards, it is likely that some acidic residues will remain which can cause long-term damage.
- By stripping away corrosion indiscriminately these treatments will remove evidence of mineral preserved organic materials, and may attack decorative elements that were hidden beneath corrosion layers.
- Foodstuffs (e.g. tomato ketchup) have unknown additives and there is no way of knowing what effect these will have on an object.

✗ Table salt

The foodstuffs described above may also contain or have sometimes been used in combination with table salt. The introduction of common household salt, sodium chloride, is the worst thing that could be done to a metal. Chlorides are a principal agent in speeding up the corrosion of metals, because they promote electrochemical activity. Experience has shown that the results of using salt are disastrous: the damage caused by table salt on a two pence piece after immersion in a saline (salt) solution for one week is clear (**colour plate 28**). Conservators have spent years trying to work out how to remove or reduce the corrosive effects of salts naturally present in corrosion products – so they may have difficulty maintaining a calm response if they hear that salt has been used as a method of cleaning! Other forms of chloride are commonly contained in many household products and these should not be used either.

Treatments which use common household salt are the worst thing that can be done to a metal object.

✗ Denture cleaning preparations (e.g. 'Steradent')

Denture cleaning preparations vary enormously in their ingredients. Commonly they will contain bicarbonate of soda, soaps and acids. They may also contain waxes, petroleum jelly, antibacterial agents, dyestuffs and flavourings. Their use can be very damaging: for example, the acids will attack both the corrosion products and the metal, and soaps will help components to dissolve (**colour plate 29**). Some may have unforeseen effects. These agents may not be removed from corrosion layers, even by careful rinsing, and could cause long-term problems in the artefact. It is difficult to design appropriate treatments to limit this damage, since the precise ingredients are not known. For all these reasons, denture cleaning liquids should be avoided at all costs.

✗ Disinfectants (e.g. 'Dettol')

Conservators of metal artefacts never use disinfectants. Disinfectants are specifically designed to destroy micro-organisms that can cause infection, not for cleaning archaeological finds. Any micro-organisms that are present on an artefact are likely to be living in any soil around the object and require water and food to grow. For this reason, most organisms are likely to be destroyed when the moisture is removed from finds when dried (see chapter 4). If artefacts are immersed in disinfectants, these will introduce moisture to the find, which will enable further corrosion to take place. They may also be acidic which can accelerate corrosion, and may introduce unknown substances into the finds which could cause problems in the longer term. Once again: avoid.

✗ Wadding (e.g. 'Silvo')

Metal cleaning wadding is easy to use and can be applied very locally, but waddings also contain an abrasive so will polish as well as clean. Not only is a high polish rarely appropriate for an archaeological object, but the action of polishing also removes minute amounts of metal. Wadding can also leave residues on the surface of an object, which would have to be removed with a solvent such as acetone. Use of wadding is not recommended for archaeological metalwork – it should only be used to clean the family silver.

✗ Liquid cleaning dips (e.g. silver dips)

Liquid cleaning dips, such as those for silver and copper alloys, contain acids and agents to carry tarnish away from the object's surface without polishing. If used on fragile archaeological silver or copper, it will not be possible to remove these acids from the corrosion layers, and they will cause further corrosion. On bright metal, they can sometimes cause re-tarnishing more quickly than usual.

Objects must never be immersed in liquid cleaner. If these products are used, they must only be considered for use if the object is robust, with solid metal under a light tarnish layer. Application should only be to small areas of an object, and all residues must be carefully removed with distilled water. The object must then be rapidly dried.

✗ Alkali treatments

Boiling in sodium hydroxide solution, suggested in some detectorist and early conservation literature as a way of removing potentially damaging chlorides from iron objects, has been shown to cause serious long-term damage to artefacts and is an extremely dangerous procedure. This technique is no longer used by conservators.

✗ Barrelling machines

Detectorists have been known to use barrelling machines (originally adapted from gemstone polishing machines) for the bulk cleaning of metal objects. Artefacts are rotated in a drum containing abrasives which remove the corrosion layers. This method is never used by professional conservators because:

- It is uncontrollable and indiscriminate (which means that it does the same amount of damage to all parts of the object inside the machine).
- The harsh abrasive and movement of the barrel will cause extensive physical damage to objects.
- It is impossible to monitor the condition of finds during the barrelling process, because it is not possible to see inside the barrel.
  The only time when it *might* be acceptable to use barrelling machines is if detectorists wish to clean post-1970 decimal coinage. But objects of archaeological significance should never be cleaned in this manner.

✗ Electrolytic cleaning

Electrolytic cleaning, or electrolysis, was more commonly employed in the past for reducing corrosion. It can only be used for reducing corrosion layers on those metal artefacts where a substantial metal core has survived and where surface detail is retained in the metal itself. In general, conservators now only use electrolysis for lead and its alloys because this soft metal can be easily scratched with manual or mechanical cleaning techniques. Using electrolytic cleaning requires experience and a thorough knowledge of chemistry. It needs to be carried out in a laboratory because of the risk of hazardous vapours which arise from the process. For these reasons, it is not recommended for use by detectorists.

✗ Cleaning coins using tin or aluminium foil

Some detectorists rub metal foil (the type which you can buy in any supermarket) on silver coins to remove tarnish. A danger with rubbing the coin is that if done repeatedly it will smooth down the surface. Also the foil can cause minute scratches on the surface. If light tarnish is to be removed it might be better to use a commercially available silver cleaning cloth.

✗ Heat treatments

The heating of any object to red heat followed by quenching (i.e. placing the object in cold water), as a means of detaching corrosion, should NEVER be carried out, as this is likely to cause considerable damage to the object and potentially to the person carrying out the treatment. The high temperatures will also completely destroy the record of the object's technological history preserved in the metallurgical structure (see chapter 3).

✗ Ultrasonic cleaning tanks

An ultrasonic tank may sometimes be used by detectorists to accelerate the action of cleaning solutions. The use of ultrasonic tanks is not recommended, particularly if used with the cleaning agents listed above. The ultrasonic action not only accelerates the cleaning action but will accelerate the damaging effects described above, not least by allowing the cleaning solution to penetrate deeper into the object.

A fragile object could also suffer physical damage if the ultrasonic action was too great.

Summary

This chapter has looked at a number of methods known to be used to clean artefacts which are either undesirable or potentially very damaging to both the object and the person doing the cleaning. For these reasons, the methods listed above are not recommended and should be avoided.

The next chapter provides advice on the different stabilisation treatments and coatings which might be used to treat objects and which of these should also be avoided.

9 Stabilisation treatments, coatings and lacquers

This chapter looks at methods which professional conservators may use to stabilise objects to help reduce further corrosion, and the pros and cons of coatings and lacquers. It also discusses coatings to avoid.

Stabilisation treatments

A change in the colour or form of the metal or corrosion may indicate that an object is actively corroding. As discussed in chapter 5, the best example of this are the bright green powdery spots, which can appear on copper alloy objects, commonly known as 'bronze disease'. Activation of corrosion like 'bronze disease' is very dependent on environmental conditions, i.e. humidity, temperature and pollutants, which is why good storage of artefacts is recommended (see also chapter 5). Prevention is always better than cure – if the object's environment is suitable for it, then the risk of these corrosion problems developing is reduced. By transferring an actively corroding object to the correct environment as soon as signs of trouble are spotted can stop it getting worse.

Very few chemical stabilisation treatments have been shown to be successful on corroded archaeological metals, which means that **storage in a dry, pollutant free, environment is normally the most effective method for controlling corrosion**. It is also advantageous, as it will not interfere with future examination or analysis of the artefact.

Where it is not possible to control its environment, an unstable copper-alloy object affected by 'bronze-disease' can be treated chemically. The only stabilisation treatment commonly used by conservators is application of the corrosion inhibitor benzotriazole (BTA), which has been shown to halt or inhibit the corrosion of unstable copper alloys. The mechanism by which it does this and the best ways to apply it are still the subject of various research projects. The object can be immersed in a dilute solution (3%) of BTA in industrial methylated spirits, but treatment seems to be more effective if this takes place under reduced air pressure (i.e. a partial vacuum) for a few hours. Such a facility is only usually available in a conservator's laboratory. Subsequent storage at below 35% RH will also help to prevent further deterioration.

Having said this, new evidence has shown that BTA may not be as reliable as previously thought and some conservators have questioned its use. It is also not fully reversible. Caution also needs to be exercised when deciding to use BTA as although it can deactivate 'bronze disease', it can also slightly change the colour of the object; green and red copper corrosion products can change in colour, and this might not be acceptable from an aesthetic viewpoint.

Health and Safety Warning

BTA may be a carcinogen (i.e. cancer-inducing) and stringent precautions should be taken in its handling and disposal. A dust mask should be worn to avoid inhaling the fine dust. Treatment with BTA should ideally be carried out in laboratory conditions and not in the home. As a hazardous chemical, BTA must not enter the environment, which means that it must not be washed down the sink. It must only be disposed of in accordance with local requirements for the disposal of hazardous waste. These requirements can be provided by your local council.

The acrylic lacquer 'Incralac' also contains BTA. There are also concerns about handling of artefacts that have been treated with BTA, which is why we recommend (chapter 6) that any objects treated with BTA have documentation indicating this kept with them.

Given that BTA is a suspected carcinogen, on balance it would be better to try and inhibit corrosion through dry storage (see chapter 5) rather than attempt to use BTA in the home.

Coatings and lacquers

Coatings and lacquers used by conservators

Coatings, or lacquers, are sometimes applied to archaeological metals to protect their surfaces from contamination, for example grease and salt transferred through handling. They may also improve the appearance of the objects, although this may be a matter of individual taste. On the downside, coatings can interfere with analysis of organic residues and may be difficult to remove. They are also not very effective at protecting the metal from further corrosion, if environmental conditions are bad, and will need to be removed if further conservation treatment is required. When a conservator does apply a coating, they try to ensure that there is complete and even coverage over the whole object, as areas left uncovered can corrode more than they would if the object was left unlacquered. However, in practice this is virtually impossible to achieve!

'Paraloid B72', an acrylic polymer, is used by conservators as a protective coating or lacquer for all archaeological metals as needed, although gold objects are rarely lacquered. A dilute solution of 'Paraloid B72' in a solvent, such as acetone, is usually applied to the surface with a soft brush. A dilute solution may also be used to penetrate further into the object in order to consolidate it, if it is very fragile and friable due to extensive corrosion. A thicker solution can also be used as an adhesive to join broken pieces. 'Paraloid B72' has been extensively tested by conservation scientists to determine how it ages; it remains relatively easy to remove with acetone and does not yellow or deteriorate over considerable periods of time.

'Incralac' is another type of acrylic lacquer. It is used by conservators to lacquer copper alloy objects which have been treated with BTA. The purpose of lacquering these objects is to prevent damage to the BTA film and also to protect those handling the objects from direct contact with BTA. 'Incralac' contains some BTA and the precautions outlined above should be taken if it is used. However once cured (hardened) the lacquered object is perfectly safe to handle.

Both 'Paraloid B72' and 'Incralac' can be purchased from specialist conservation suppliers, such as those listed in Appendix 3.

Coatings to avoid
✗ Waxes (e.g. beeswax), petroleum jelly and boot polish

Various types of wax have been used over the years as coatings and consolidants for metal objects. Conservators sometimes do apply protective waxes (e.g. 'Renaissance wax') to objects such as historical sculptures, particularly to outdoor metalwork, if they have a solid, uncorroded surface and if a hard slightly shiny finish, which can be 'buffed' up, is required. However, such a surface coating is generally unsuitable for an archaeological metal object, particularly those where traces of organic remains may be preserved within the corrosion layers. Even if they survived the application of the wax, once clogged up with it their structures will be virtually impossible to identify. In the past, when conservators had no alternative, beeswax was used as a consolidant for fragile archaeological objects; nowadays synthetic polymers such as 'Paraloid B72' are preferred. Once applied, waxes and petroleum jelly are very difficult to remove. They can also trap moisture against the surface of the object which can promote further corrosion. 'Vaseline' and some waxes stay tacky and will also trap dust and dirt on the surface of the object. Furthermore, petroleum jelly, most waxes and boot polish all contain unknown additives – manufacturers rarely give out their recipes and it is not known what effects these will have on an object in years to come. **Colour plate 30** clearly shows the harmful effects of boot polish on a two pence coin; unstable components in the polish have caused corrosion to start, visible in the form of green spots.

All these substances are therefore best avoided.

✗ Oils (e.g. olive oil, neatsfoot (sump) oil and 'WD-40')

Some metal detector users favour coating their objects with an oil, often olive oil, with the intention of stopping their finds corroding. This is not recommended: oiling an object will not keep moisture out completely. Moreover, the practice of boiling objects in oil in an effort to drive off air is equally ineffective, as damp air can still penetrate and cause corrosion of the surfaces beneath. Any heat treatment may also alter the structure of the metal at a microscopic level.

Experience in the conservation of oil-treated objects has also shown that complete removal of the oil is almost impossible, and the surface beneath may become 'sugary' in texture and disintegrate. Conservation of such a surface is extremely difficult. Oils also interfere with the potential for analysis of organic residues.

Although oils might give an attractive appearance to a metal object in the short term, their ability to preserve it in the long term is extremely poor and can make the condition of an object far worse than before. Thus, once again, these substances should be avoided.

Summary

This chapter has looked at some ways in which conservators try to stabilise and protect objects, and discussed some of the substances which should not be used. The next chapter looks at the three 'r's, namely repair, reconstruction and restoration.

10 Repair, reconstruction and restoration

This chapter looks at some of the methods used by professional conservators to repair, reconstruct and restore metal artefacts and factors which guide their use.

In relation to archaeological metal objects, reattaching a part that has broken off would be to repair the object. If the object was in many pieces which could be joined together, this would be termed reconstruction. If the conservator then went on to fill missing areas of the reconstructed object, this might then be termed restoration. An additional type of restoration is reshaping, whereby a metal object is manipulated to return it to its original form. However, such restoration – by a conservator of archaeological objects – always stops well short of trying to make the object look as it did when new.

Objects might be repaired, reconstructed or restored in order to make them safer to handle and study and to make them more understandable to the viewer; an object reconstructed from many different pieces is likely to make more sense, to be more recognisable as an object, than a pile of fragments.

When deciding how to repair, reconstruct or restore an object a conservator has to take account of several factors. The first of these is reversibility – i.e. ensuring that it will be possible to undo the joins or remove the fills in missing areas, without damaging the original parts of the object. It may be necessary to undo such work because new original pieces are found which then have to be fitted in. Another reason might be because after further study and research, it is decided that the original shape of the object is different to that of the restoration. This happened with the Sutton Hoo helmet, which was restored in 1949, and then dismantled and restored again in 1969-70, following further research by archaeologists into the likely shape of the helmet. The story of the restoration and re-restoration of the Sutton Hoo helmet is described in a chapter by Nigel Williams in the book *The Art of the Conservator* (Oddy 1992).

Another issue is one that seems obvious to conservators and archaeologists, but may not necessarily be obvious to others. A part will only be reattached if the conservator is certain it originally belonged to that object. In museums, to repair an object with a part from a different object, even if very similar, is considered to be unethical, as it would create an object that had never existed and would consequently be considered to be at least misleading and at most a forgery. It is interesting, however, that people did not hold this view in the eighteenth or early nineteenth centuries, when the creation of such objects – which are technically termed pastiches – was a common restoration practice.

Repair and reconstruction

Adhesives, used to join parts of an object together, need to be reversible and to remain so for a long time. Two adhesives that conservators often use and which are suitable for most metal objects are an acrylic adhesive based on 'Paraloid B72' and 'HMG', a cellulose nitrate adhesive (for suppliers, see Appendix 3). The good thing about these adhesives is that acetone can be used to undo a join. If this is applied, on a soft paintbrush, along the glued join line, the adhesive should dissolve, allowing the joined parts to be separated again. Care is taken not to pull pieces apart until the adhesive is thoroughly softened, otherwise some of the break edge may be pulled away.

These totally reversible adhesives, however, may not have the strength to hold a joint in a large heavy object. If there is a risk of damage to the object, should the repaired join fail, a conservator may decide that the physical security of the object, in the long term, outweighs the importance of using a reversible adhesive. If stronger repairs are required, an epoxy resin like 'Araldite' might be used even though they are not easily undone without risk to the object, and mistakes are thus difficult to rectify.

When deciding which adhesive to use, conservators also aim to always use an adhesive which is slightly weaker than the object so that if the object is put under stress, then the join will fail rather than the object. If fragments to be joined are very fragile or corroded, they might be consolidated before joins are made. A dilute solution of an acrylic adhesive (e.g. 'Paraloid B72') could be used as a consolidant.

High street adhesives – for example, instant glues – should not be used for two reasons. Firstly, they may contain ingredients which are harmful to archaeological objects and secondly, they could create a join which is virtually impossible to undo.

Restoration

Missing areas in a reconstructed object may be filled to give additional structural stability to the object, or to make it easier to understand. Again, reversible materials are used for gap fills. Conservators often prefer to make their own gap filler; for example, an acrylic adhesive might be used, thickened with inert fillers such as tiny glass beads or 'microballoons'. If a stronger gap fill is needed, an epoxy resin based filler, or a polyester paste such as 'plastic padding' might be used. A coat of lacquer is first painted onto the edges of the area being filled as a separating layer between the metal (or corrosion) and the filler.

Once it has cured (hardened), a filled area might be painted to tone it in with the surrounding surface of the original object. Acrylic paints or powder pigments in an acrylic medium might be used to paint gap-fills. Care is taken to ensure that none of the paint is allowed to get on the actual object. This is because in museum restoration work, it is important that the viewer should always be able to tell which parts are the original object and which the new filled areas – and also because you do not want to paint archaeological objects!

Health and Safety Warning
Epoxy resins, polyester resins, and the solvents used in acrylic and HMG adhesives, all present a potential health and safety hazard for the user. Gloves (nitrile) should be worn when handling these substances and they should only be used in a well ventilated area, ideally in a fume cupboard.

Restoration by reshaping
A different type of restoration to gap filling is that of reshaping or manipulating a metal object in order to return it to something approaching its original form. All metal detector users will know that finds are often misshapen when discovered, particularly as metal objects in the upper soil levels are far more likely to have been knocked and dented by ploughs and rotivators.

It might come as a surprise to learn that reshaping is rarely considered an option by professional conservators except in some very exceptional circumstances. This is for two main reasons. The first is the condition of the metal. Successful reshaping by, for example, realigning bent parts or pushing out and smoothing a dent, will only be possible if the metal has retained its malleability after centuries of burial, but this is rarely the case. To the naked eye, the condition of the metal might look good, but if it has become brittle with 'intergranular' corrosion only visible at a microscopic level, the metal will no longer be malleable and would break if reshaping was attempted.

The only possible exception might be silver objects, because it may be possible to restore the malleability of silver sufficiently enough to allow reshaping. To do this the object is first heated (annealed). While this might restore enough malleability to reshape it, the heat will destroy any evidence of the original working techniques used on the object which are preserved at a microscopic level. There is also a great risk that the metal could melt, thereby destroying the object.

Even if the metal's condition makes reshaping a possibility, the other reason for not doing it is because the bends and dents could be a very important part of the history of that object and are therefore important to keep. Some objects were deliberately broken or damaged in antiquity before being buried, for example as part of a votive offering. In prehistoric periods in Britain, weapons and tools were often deliberately bent at the end of their working life, perhaps as a way of allowing the 'spirit' of the object to be released. In such circumstances, any such damage would be considered as part of the history of the object, and the view taken by archaeologists would be that the object should be preserved as discovered.

In general, any attempts to reshape objects should ideally be avoided.

Summary

This chapter has looked at some of the techniques used to repair and reconstruct objects where appropriate, and also discusses the issue of reshaping, something which is rarely carried out by professional conservators. The next chapter will look at the best way to display objects, which detectorists often wish to do.

11 Displaying objects

Metal detector users often want to display their objects, and do so for a variety of reasons. At home finders may like to display their most cherished and exciting finds, but like museums, have only a small part of their collections on display at any one time. Detector groups may display finds at local fairs and fêtes as a way of showing their discoveries to their local community, or might even be involved in competitions with other rival groups to come up with the most exciting displays of finds.

As with all the advice given in this book there is good and bad practice, from the conservation viewpoint, when displaying objects. There are good and bad display materials which can be used. The main problem is that some materials can give off substances (for example, organic acid gases emitted by some woods), which will cause metals to actively corrode.

Recommended display materials and methods

Museums across the country, and indeed around the world, have a wide variety of ways in which artefacts, and information about them, can be presented in display cases. These may include information panels and labels, perhaps accompanied by maps, photographs and illustrations, as well as the objects. The objects might be mounted on boards using either pins, pegs, or brackets, or simply laid flat at the bottom of the display case. All museums should be trying to ensure that their objects are well maintained from a conservation point of view when on display, and we would encourage metal detector users to feel that they have a similar responsibility towards our heritage. So whether objects are in a museum or in private hands, there are two main conservation principles which need to be addressed when it comes to their display:

1. Any materials which come into contact with, or are close to, objects must not cause them harm. This applies to any materials used for display cases, display boards, or supports for the objects. In museums the possible effects of paint and floor coverings, particularly in a new gallery, are also checked before selecting materials which are safe to use.

2. The environment needs to be suitable for the objects in question, which in most cases (especially metalwork) will mean dry (see chapter 5).

The following suggestions on how to display objects and which materials to use are intended to help detectorists to safely mount displays of their objects at home.

Good display practice

1. Display boards can be made from perspex or 'Plastazote' foam and can be covered with a backing cloth of undyed polyester, cotton or linen. The former can be purchased from specialist conservation suppliers (see Appendix 3), whilst suitable textiles can be found in high street haberdashers. Dyed textiles, or those which have a special surface finish, have been found to be more likely to cause metals to corrode so undyed, unfinished cotton or linen (such as unbleached calico) is likely to be the safest option (**colour plate 31**).

2. Alternatively, wood may be used for display boards, but should be coated with an emulsion paint, or sealed in aluminium foil before being covered with a backing cloth. It is important that the aluminium foil covering is not pierced if used. However, wood is not recommended for use with lead objects, even if covered, as lead is particularly vulnerable to corrosion caused by organic acids from wood.

3. Ideally, objects should be displayed flat as this is most likely to give them even support. If the board slopes, then perspex pegs or brackets and plastic covered pins are recommended to support the object. An example of different types of pins used to support coins, showing good and bad practice, is provided in **colour plate 32**.

It is important to ensure that any weak areas of an object are well supported, and not put under any undue stress. It is also important to ensure that the size of the support is appropriate for the weight and nature of the object to prevent it being marked or otherwise damaged. For example, a heavy object with a soft fragile corroded surface resting on just a couple of uncovered metal pins will probably be found to have the impression of the pins indented into its surface when taken off display.

4. Placing objects inside a display case will help keep the dust off them. Also, if the display case can be sealed to be as airtight as possible, then a controlled environment can be created inside the case to prevent further corrosion (as in a storage box described in chapter 5). Glass and perspex are safe materials out of which to construct a display case. However, some types of wood (see below) should be avoided. The best method of sealing a display case will depend on its construction and the type of objects being displayed. A conservator can advise on methods for sealing cases (see Appendix 3). If a sealant is used this should be an alcohol curing silicone, rather than one which gives off harmful acetic acid as it cures.

5. If a dry environment inside the display case needs to be created, this can be achieved by placing a bag of silica gel in the box or cabinet (see chapter 5 for the amount of silica gel to use in different size boxes), but this will only work if the display case is airtight.

6. If the correct environment cannot be maintained, vulnerable objects should be displayed for a limited time only, and then returned to dry storage.

7. It is important to ensure that displays are sited well away from sources of heat, such as hot tungsten lights, radiators or direct sunlight. Some damage may be caused to metal objects if they are repeatedly heated and cooled rapidly.

Display materials and methods to avoid

There are many types of display materials which can be harmful to finds, and some of these are listed below.

- Some natural woods (such as oak), chipboard or other wood composites should be avoided for constructing display boards or cases, because they can give off harmful acids and formaldehydes that can cause corrosion. Lead and lead alloy artefacts are particularly susceptible to organic acids and are best stored and displayed well away from any wood. This even includes sealed or covered wood.
- Animal fibres like silk and wool also give off harmful substances which can corrode or tarnish metals. Textiles made of silk or wool (e.g. felt) should be avoided.
- PVC plastic, polyurethane lacquers and white, water-based glues should also be avoided, as they all contain harmful pollutants.
- Nylon thread is not recommended for long-term display, as it can deteriorate and break in the heat of display lights. The condition of any brackets or supports for objects should be checked regularly and replaced if they show any sign of deterioration.
- The following should NEVER be used for holding objects: drawing pins, nails, staples, 'blu-tack', modelling clay, adhesive tapes or any other type of adhesive. Adhesives, 'blu-tack' and modelling clay can leave sticky residues and stain artefacts – such residues and stains may be difficult, if not impossible to remove.

Summary

This chapter has provided advice on how finds can be displayed, and has also provided a list of materials and methods which should be avoided as they can be very harmful to archaeological objects.

PART III: APPENDICES

Appendix 1
Metal detecting in England and Wales

Metal detecting is a legal activity in England and Wales. Scotland and Ireland have different laws relating to detecting and the ownership and reporting of archaeological material; for example, in Scotland, *bona vacantia* requires that all archaeological finds are reported to the Secretary of the Treasure Trove Advisory Panel; in Northern Ireland there is also a statutory duty to report all archaeological finds.

Although metal detecting is not illegal, detectorists nonetheless have both legal and moral obligations to ensure that the archaeological material which they discover is properly reported and cared for. This book is principally concerned with conservation issues relating to archaeological metalwork found; this appendix provides important additional information about how the hobby should be conducted in order that these legal and moral obligations are met.

1. Be aware of reporting obligations

Treasure and wreck material must be reported if discovered, and information about these laws is given below. Finders are also strongly urged to voluntarily report their objects under the Portable Antiquities Scheme, which is also discussed in more detail below.

2. Join a national representative body

Detector users are strongly advised to become members of national bodies which represent their interests and can provide advice on carrying out their hobby responsibly through their respective Codes of Conduct. Both these organisations accept individual members; the other alternative is to join a local metal detecting club, which will usually be affiliated to one of these organisations. These bodies also provide members with the necessary personal liability insurance which is needed before any detecting takes place.

There are two national organisations in the UK which detectorists can join, either as individuals or as members of metal detecting clubs. These organisations are:
The National Council for Metal Detecting (NCMD)
Contact: Trevor Austin, 51 Hill Top Gardens, Denaby, Doncaster, DN12 4SA.
Website: www.ncmd.co.uk

Federation of Independent Detectorists (FID)
Contact: Colin Hanson, Detector Lodge, 44 Heol Dulais, Birchgrove, Swansea, West
Glamorgan, SA7 9LT.
Website: www.newbury.net/fid

3. Always obtain landowner's permission before metal detecting

Any metal detecting on land in England and Wales should only be conducted after
permission has been given to do so. All land in the UK, including beaches, has an owner,
and permission to metal detect – which we strongly advise is provided in writing – should
always be obtained in advance. For privately owned land, this is potentially straightforward (although bear in mind that the land occupier might be different to the owner), and
once again metal detecting clubs and the national bodies can provide information. There
are however two other types of land which are governed by different legal requirements:

a. Scheduled Ancient Monuments: these are designated areas of archaeological importance
   overseen by English Heritage in England and Cadw in Wales. It is an offence to use a
   metal detector on a Scheduled site without the written agreement of the Secretary of
   State.
b. Areas of Archaeological Importance: in England these are all areas of the historical
   towns York, Hereford, Chester, Exeter and Canterbury. Once again, it is an offence to
   remove any archaeological objects from land within these areas.

Detectorists should also be aware that common land, such as parks and foreshore areas,
are likely to be subject to local council bylaws which vary greatly across the country.
Therefore before any detecting is carried out on these areas the local council should be
contacted for advice.

4. Ensure that there is agreement regarding ownership of finds

If permission has been obtained from the landowner, it is important to ensure that
agreement is reached regarding ownership of finds. This is particularly important in
relation to any treasure which is discovered; most detectorists agree that any rewards paid
for such objects are divided equally between themselves and the landowner.

5. Only detect on disturbed ploughland and not deeper than plough depth

Undisturbed land, for example pasture, should be left undug. This is because there may
be archaeological layers underneath in which all the finds are in context; such sites are
increasingly rare in Britain and should only be excavated by professional archaeologists if
the need arises (usually ahead of development). If metal detecting is carried out, it is
better that this is done on disturbed ploughsoil, as the objects are no longer in their
original archaeological context. But even here, known archaeological sites, particularly
newly discovered ones, ought to be avoided. And all finds made in ploughsoil should be
reported; see below.

The Treasure Act

In 1997 the Treasure Act came into force. This was a revision of the very ancient law of Treasure Trove (earliest references to this date back to about the twelfth century). When anyone in England or Wales finds treasure, they are required to report it by law.

The following rules are used to decide whether an object is treasure or not:

- All finds containing at least 10% of gold or silver, which are more than 300 years old, along with any associated objects (whatever they are made of), qualify as treasure.

For coins, the rules are slightly different:

- For coins which are more than 300 years old and contain at least 10% gold or silver, then any two or more coins found together, along with any associated artefacts, qualify as treasure.
- For coins which are more than 300 years old but contain less that 10% gold or silver, then any 10 or more coins found together, along with any associated artefacts, qualify as treasure.

Finally, any objects which would have been Treasure Trove, but do not fall under the specific categories given above, are also treasure. These are objects made substantially of silver or gold that have been buried with the intention of recovery and whose owners or their heirs cannot be traced.

Objects whose owners can be traced, unworked natural objects even if found in association with treasure and single coins, or found on their own, do not qualify as treasure.

Finders should also be aware that in November 2001, following a review of the Treasure Act, the Government announced its intention to bring an Order to revise the definition of treasure to include (a) deposits of prehistoric base metal objects and (b) all prehistoric objects, any part of which contains gold or silver. This Order is to be introduced into Parliament in summer 2002, together with a revised Code of Practice, and it is expected that they will come into force in January 2003.

What should someone do if they find treasure?

Finders are legally required to report any find which may qualify as treasure to the coroner for the district in which it was found **either** within two weeks of the day on which they made the find **or** within two weeks of the day on which they realised that the find might be treasure.

It is sometimes difficult to recognise gold or silver when they have been alloyed with more base metals as the corrosion will be characteristic of the less stable metals within the alloy. If there is any doubt as to whether an artefact is made from gold or silver, it should be taken to the local finds liaison officer, local museum or reported to the coroner for the district.

Copies of both the Code of Practice on the Treasure Act and a leaflet that explains the Act can be obtained free of charge from either your local finds liaison officer or from the Department for Culture Media and Sport (tel. 0207 211 6200). Information can also be found on the web at: www.culture.gov.uk.

No cleaning or reshaping should be undertaken before a find is reported and submitted for examination to a museum as instructed by the coroner.

The find(s) should be packed carefully to avoid physical damage or damage by abrasion. In addition, no attempt should be made to excavate hoards of coins or other objects if discovered. Readers are referred to chapter 5 in this book for further information.

The Portable Antiquities Scheme

To complement the Treasure Act, the Portable Antiquities Scheme was introduced in 1997 (also known as 'Finding our Past'). This is a voluntary scheme to encourage amateur finders, and in particular metal detector users, to report all their finds for recording, in addition to any treasure discoveries which have to be reported by law. At the time of writing, there are 12 finds liaison officers covering about half of England and Wales (see Appendix 3). In 2003 26 new finds liaison officer posts will be created, giving a complete coverage of all of England and Wales. For more information, please visit the website at: www.finds.org.uk, or contact:

The Portable Antiquities Scheme Outreach Officer, c/o Dept. of Coins and Medals, The British Museum, London WC1B 3DG.

A leaflet about the Scheme as well as other information can be provided free of charge.
A full list of contacts for the regional finds liaison officers with the Portable Antiquities Scheme is also provided in Appendix 3.

Wreck

The Treasure Act and the Portable Antiquities Scheme only apply to finds made on land in England and Wales. For underwater finds made anywhere in UK territorial waters, different laws apply and finders need to be aware of these.
Wreck is defined as anything which is found in or on the sea, or washed ashore from tidal water. **All** items which are raised, regardless of age or importance, must be reported to the Receiver of Wreck.
For more information, finders are advised to contact:

The Receiver of Wreck, Bay 1/05, Spring Place, 105 Commercial Road, Southampton SO15 1EG.

Alternatively finders can look on the web at: www.mcagency.org.

Appendix 2
Taking a map reference

Making a note of where finds have been discovered is a very important part of the process of the discovery of objects, and finders are strongly encouraged to do so (more information is provided in chapter 4). Some finders may wish to use handheld Global Positioning System (GPS) devices, which will give very accurate findspot information, and we would encourage finders to use these if they can. Failing that, this section explains how to take a grid reference from an Ordnance Survey map which is less accurate than a GPS but better than not doing so at all. We would advise using either 1:50,000 scale or 1:25,000 scale maps, and finders should provide information to an accuracy of at least six figures if possible.

Using the National Grid

Taking a National Grid reference is very straightforward if the following steps are followed. In the example below, a six-figure grid reference is the result, which provides an accuracy of $100m^2$. Ideally an eight-figure grid reference should be provided for all finds, but this is unlikely to be possible to assess accurately in the field.

To take a reference, the following steps should be followed:

1. The whole of the UK is divided into 100km grid squares, each with a 2 letter code (e.g. 'TL'). So the first part of a reference consists of these two letters; they can be found within their relevant area on all ordnance survey maps, or on the corner of the map.
2. The next step is to find the 10km grid square in which your site is located. This is done by taking the easting (the vertical lines which run from left to right across the map) and then the northing (the horizontal lines which run from the bottom of the map to the top). So follow the simple numbers along the bottom from 0 to 9 and then do the same counting from bottom to top. Some people remember this by saying 'Along the hall, THEN up the stairs'.
3. On most maps, however, the grid has probably been divided up even further into 1km grid squares for you. Thus by using the same principle outlined in step 2, you should be able to read off the 1km grid square you are located in very easily – for example, 'TL6836'. This will provide you with a four-figure grid reference accurate to a 1km square.
4. To take things one step further and to give your finds a decent level of findspot accuracy, it is then possible to estimate within the grid square to an accuracy of six figures ($100m^2$). This can be done very simply by using the same principle as before; simply start with the easting, e.g. '683' (three-tenths of the way across from the 68 line running south the north), and then count upwards in the same manner, e.g. '365' (halfway up the grid square numbered 36 at the side of the map). Put it all together, and you have a six-figure grid reference: 'TL683365'.

The Ordnance Survey also provide a free information sheet for recording national grid references. This can be obtained by calling their helpline on 08456 050505, or visiting their website at: www.ordsvy.org.uk.

Appendix 3
Contacts and suppliers

Much of the information provided in this guide is practical advice on how objects can be looked after in the field and subsequently the home. However, in a number of instances it is strongly advisable to seek additional help, either with excavating finds in the field or looking after them properly when problems arise. Local museum curators should be able to help, and you should be able to find their contact details in your local phone book. They should be able to put you in touch with professional archaeological conservators.

Another source of guidance are the finds liaison officers with the Portable Antiquities Scheme (see Appendix 1), and a full list of contacts for these is provided below. From 2003, there will be more officers based across England and Wales, and for information on these new officers finders are advised to contact the outreach officer or look on: www.finds.org.uk.

Outreach Officer

Portable Antiquities Outreach Officer, c/o Dept. of Coins & Medals, British Museum, London WC1B 3DG. Tel.: 0207 323 8611.

Regional Finds Liaison Officers

Dorset & Somerset
Finds Liaison Officer, Somerset Museum Service, The Castle, Castle Green, Taunton, Somerset TA1 4AA. Tel.: 01823 320200.
Also at: Archaeological Service, Environmental Services, Directorate, County Hall, Colliton Park, Dorchester DT1 1XJ. Tel.: 01305 224921.

Hampshire
Finds Liaison Officer, Hyde Historical Resource Centre, 75 Hyde Street, Winchester, Hants. SO23 7DW. Tel.: 01962 848269.

Kent
Finds Liaison Officer, Heritage Conservation, Kent County Council, Invicta House, Maidstone, Kent ME14 1XX Tel.: 01622 221544.

Norfolk
Finds Liaison Officer, Identification & Recording, Norfolk Museums Service, Union House, Gressenhall, Dereham, Norfolk NR20 4DR. Tel.: 01362 869031.

North Lincolnshire
Finds Liaison Officer, North Lincolnshire District Museum, Oswald Road, Scunthorpe, Lincolnshire DN15 7BD. Tel.: 01724 843533.

The North-West
(Cheshire, Cumbria, Greater Manchester, Lancashire and Merseyside)
Finds Liaison Officer, Liverpool Museum, William Brown Street, Liverpool L3 8EN. Tel.: 0151 478 4259.

Northamptonshire
Finds Liaison Officer, Northamptonshire Heritage, PO Box 163, County Hall, Northampton NN1 1AX. Tel.: 01604 237249.

Suffolk
Finds Liaison Officer, Suffolk County Council, Archaeology Section, Shire Hall, Bury St Edmunds, Suffolk IP33 2AR. Tel.: 01284 352449.

Wales: Finds co-ordinator
Finds Co-ordinator, Department of Archaeology & Numismatics, National Museum & Galleries of Wales, Cathays Park, Cardiff CF1 3NP. Tel.: 02920 573226.

The West Midlands (southern Staffordshire, northern Warwickshire, West Midlands and Worcestershire)
Finds Liaison Officer, Birmingham Museum & Art Gallery, Chamberlain Square, Birmingham B3 3DH. Tel.: 0121 303 4636.

Yorkshire
Finds Liaison Officer, The Yorkshire Museum, Museum Gardens, York, Yorkshire YO1 2DR. Tel.: 01904 629745.

Some sources of conservation advice

Finders may also if they wish contact professional conservators directly. However, finders should be aware that professional conservators cannot give out specific advice relating to the cleaning and conservation of finds over the telephone or by correspondence.

United Kingdom Institute for Conservation (Archaeology Section), 109 The Chandlery, 50 Westminster Bridge Road, London SE1 7QY. Tel.: 020 7721 8721. Website: www.ukic.org.uk.

Department of Conservation, The British Museum, Great Russell Street, London WC1B 3DG Tel.: 020 7323 8678; fax 020 7323 8636. email: conservation@thebritishmuseum.ac.uk.

National Museums & Galleries of Wales, Cathays Park, Cardiff CF1 3NP. Tel.: 01222 397951; fax 01222 373219.

Museum of London, London Wall, London EC2Y 5HN. Tel.: 020 7600 3699; fax 020 7600 1058 (can provide advice on finds from the London area).

National Museums and Galleries on Merseyside, The Conservation Centre, Whitechapel, Liverpool, L1 6HZ. Tel.: 0151 207 0001.

Conservators based in local museums via Yellow Pages or via Regional Museums Councils:

Council of Museums in Wales, The Courtyard, Letty Street, Cathays, Cardiff CF2 4EL. Tel.: 029 2022 5432.
East Midlands Museums Service, PO Box 7221, Nottingham NG12 3WH. Tel.: 01949 981734.
London Museums Agency, Cloister Court, 22-26 Farringdon Lane, London EC1R 3AJ. Tel.: 020 7549 1700.
North of England Museums, Libraries and Archives Council (NEMLAC), House of Recovery, Bath Lane, Newcastle upon Tyne NE4 5S. Tel.: 0191 222 1661.
North West Museums Service, Griffin Lodge, Griffin Park, Cavendish Place, Blackburn BB2 2PN. Tel.: 01254 670211.
South East Museums, Libraries and Archives Council (SEMLAC), 8 City Business Centre, Hyde Street, Winchester, Hants. SO23 7TA. Tel.: 01962 844909.
also at: The Garden Room, Historic Dockyard, Chatham, Kent ME4 4TE. Tel.: 01634 405301.
South West Museums, Libraries and Archives Council, Creech Castle, Bathpool, Taunton TA1 2DX. Tel.: 01823 259696.
West Midlands Museums Service, Hanbury Road, Stoke Prior, Bromsgove B60 4AD. Tel.: 01527 872258.
Yorkshire Museums Council, Farnley Hall, Hall Lane, Farnley Park, Leeds LS12 5HA. Tel.: 0113 263 8909.

The Regional Museums Councils are overseen by Resource: Council for Museums, Archives and Libraries, 16 Queen Annes Gate, London SW16 9AA. Tel.: 020 7273 1444. Website: www.resource.gov.uk.

Finds officers and conservators with local archaeological units from:

Institute of Field Archaeologists (Finds Group), c/o IFA University of Reading, 2 Earley Gate, PO Box 239, Reading, RG6 6AU. Tel.: 0118 9316446. Website: www.archaeologists.net.
English Heritage (London based as well as regional conservators), Ancient Monuments Laboratory, 23 Savile Row, London, W1X 1AB. Tel.: 0207 973 3000. Website: www.english-heritage.org.uk.
Nautical Archaeology Society, c/o Mary Rose Trust, College Road, H M Naval Base, Portsmouth PO1 3LX. Tel.: 01705 750521; fax 01705 870588.

Suppliers of packaging for storage of archaeological finds

Suitable packing materials and other products for conservation have been discussed throughout this book, and sources of supply for materials have been indicated in the text as necessary. Some of the items mentioned can be found in the local high street (for instance, polythene storage boxes), other materials are more specialised and will need to be bought from specialist suppliers.

In the first instance, finders are advised to look in their local Yellow Pages for suppliers of packing materials, and finds liaison officers and local museums should also be able to advise. When buying conservation products, it is worth getting together with fellow detectorists if at all possible, as many retailers will tend to sell products only in bulk. In addition to local suppliers, the list below provides details for a number of retailers of products mentioned in the text. Some of these will not sell to private individuals, but should be able to provide advice on where their products can be obtained locally.

Materials

Acid free tissue paper	*Atlantis; Conservation by Design*
Permanent 'Artline' pens	*Roman Press Ltd; stationary suppliers*
Relative Humidity indicator strips	*Conservation Resources;*
	Preservation Equipment Ltd.;
	Sud Chemie (UK) Ltd.
Polyethylene foam (e.g. 'Jiffy' foam)	*National Packaging Ltd;*
	Jiffy Packaging Ltd.
Self seal polyethylene bags	*Conservation Resources;*
	local packaging suppliers
Polythene foam (= 'Plasatzote')	*Plasmar Ltd; Zotefoams* (wholesale only)
Polystyrene boxes	*The Stewart Company* (but only wholesale)
Polythene boxes	*The Stewart Company* (but only wholesale)
Silica gel	*Gee Jay Chemicals Ltd (only wholesale);*
	Conservation Resources
Polythene labels (e.g. 'Tyvek')	*Conservation Resources*
Bubble wrap	Local packaging suppliers
Perspex mounts for display	*Dauphin Display*
Adhesives ('Paraloid B72' &	*Conservation Resources; H Marcel Guest Ltd.*
Cellulose Nitrate adhesives)	

Contact details for the suppliers listed above

Atlantis European Ltd.

7/9 Plummers Row, London, EC1 1EQ
Tel.: 020 7377 8855; fax: 020 7377 8850

Conservation by Design

5 Singer Way, Woburn Road Industrial Estate, Kempston, Beds. MK42 7AW
Tel.: 01234 853555; website: www.conservationby-design.co.uk

Conservation Resources (UK) Ltd

Units 1,2 & 4 Pony Road, Horspath Industrial Estate, Cowley Oxfordshire, OX4 2RD
Tel.: 01865 747755; e-mail: vpackthread@aol.com

Dauphin Display
PO Box 602, East Oxford, OX44 9LU
Tel.: 01865 343542; fax: 01865 343307

Gee Jay Chemicals Ltd
16 Gosforth Close, Middlefield Industrial Estate, Sandy, Beds, SG19 1RB
Tel.: 01767 682774; website: www.geejaychemicals.co.uk

H Marcel Guest Ltd
Riverside Works, Collyhurst Road, Manchester M40 7RU
Tel.: 0161 205 7631

Jiffy Packaging Co. Ltd
Industrial Estate, Winsford, Cheshire, CW7 3QY
Tel.: 01606 551221; website: www.pactiv.com

National Packaging Ltd
Trinity Works, Lockfield Avenue, Brimsdown, Enfield, Middlesex EN3 7PY
Tel.: 020 8805 3333

Plasmar Ltd
Neachells Lane, Wednesfield, Wolverhampton, West Midlands, WV11 3QG
Tel.: 01902 307711; email: sales@beldanplasmar.com

Preservation Equipment Ltd
Vinces Road, Diss, Norfolk, IP22 4HQ
Tel.: 020 8681 0311

Roman Press Ltd
19 Woodside Road, Southbourne, Bournemouth, BH5 2BA
Tel.: 01202 424222; website: email: statsales@theromangroup.co.uk

The Stewart Company
Stewart House, Waddon Marsh Way, Purley Way, Croydon, CR9 4HS
Tel.: 020 8686 2231; www.stewartcompany.co.uk

Sud Chemie (UK) Ltd
Dalton Way, Middlewich Business Park, Middlewich, Cheshire LW10 0HO
Tel.: 01606 813060

Zotefoams
675 Mitcham Road, Croydon, Surrey CR9 3AL
Tel.: 020 8664 1600

Appendix 4
Further reading

Bradley, S. (ed.) *A Guide to the Storage, Exhibition and Handling of Antiquities*, Ethnographia and Pictorial Art, BMP Occasional Paper no.66, 1990

Cronyn, J. *The Elements of Archaeological Conservation*, Routledge, London, 1990

Goodburn-Brown, D. & UKICAS *Excavated Artefacts and Conservation*, Conservation Guidelines No. 1, UKICAS, 2001

Payton, R. *The Retrieval of Objects from Archaeological Sites*, Archetype Publications, London, 1992

Robinson, W. *First Aid for Underwater Finds*, Archetype, London, 1998

Sease, C. *A Conservation Manual for the Field Archaeologist*, UCLA IA Art Volume 4, Los Angeles, 1987

Tylecote, R.F. *The Prehistory of Metallurgy in the British Isles*, The Institute of Metals, 1986

Walker, K. *Guidelines for the Preparation of Excavation Archives for Long term Storage*, United Kingdom Institute for Conservation Archaeology Section, 1990

Watkins, S. & Enderly, C. 'Processing Coin Hoards at the British Museum' in Goodburn-Brown & Jones. (eds) *Look after the Pennies*, Archetype Publications Ltd, London,1998

Watkinson, D. & Neal, V. *First Aid for Finds*, Rescue and United Kingdom Institute for Conservation Archaeology Section, 3rd edition, 1997

Williams, N. 'The Sutton Hoo Helmet' in Oddy, A. (ed.) *The Art of the Conservator*, British Museum Publications, pp.73-88, 1992

Index

Numbers in **bold** refer to figures

abrasives, 55, 69
abrasive powders, 15, 60
acetic acid, *see* acids
acetone, 62, 68, 73, 76
acids, 24, 38-9, 68, 81
  acetic acid, 66, 80
  citric acid, 63, 66
  formic acid, 63
  hydrochloric acid, 63
  organic acids, 24, 63, 79, 81
  phosphoric acid, 66
  sulphuric acid, 63
acid free tissue, **10**, 44-6, 90,
  colour plate 12
acidic vapours, 44
acrylic adhesives, *see* adhesives
acrylic lacquer, 72
acrylic paints, 77
acrylic polymer, 73
active corrosion, 23, 41, 49-50,
  colour plates 14-18
adhesives, 55, 76, 90
  acrylic adhesives, 76-7
  cellulose nitrate adhesives, 76, 90
aerobic soils, 25
air-abrasive machine, 60
airing cupboard, 41, 47
alcohol curing silicone, 80
alkali treatments, 69
alkaline, 30
alloys, 12-13, 16, 21, 39
aluminium, 12
  aluminium foil, 30, 70, 80
amber, 47
analytical techniques, 53
Anglo-Saxon, 18, 52, **colour
  plates 7-8, 19-23**
animal fibres, 81
annealing, 12-13, 15-16, 77
antibacterial agents, 68
antimony, 18
antler, 54
'Araldite', 76
Areas of Archaeological
  Importance, 83
armour, 18
'Artline' pens, 24, **4**
azurite, **colour plate 2**

backing cloth, 80
bacteria, 26, 55
ballpoint pens, 45
barrelling machines, 69
base metals, 14, 20, 22, 39, 84
beaches, 83
beads, 14-15, 17
bed frames, 18
beeswax, 73
bellows, 13
belt straps, 54
benzotriazole (BTA), 56, 71-3
bicarbonate of soda, 68
blacksmiths, 19
blisters, 24
bloom, 19
'blu tack', 81
blue corrosion, 25, 54
bona vacantia, 82
bone, 7, 26-7, 30, 42, 47,
  colour plate 4
boot polish, 73, **colour plate 30**
brackets, 81
brass, 16, 40, 54
bristle brushes, 66
Britannia metal, *see* pewter
brittle, 12, 15-16, 19, 24, 37, 58, 77
bronze, 16, 18, 40
  Bronze Age, 15, 17, 18
  'bronze disease', 21, 23, 49, 71-
  2, **colour plates 17-18**
brooches, 16, 22, 26, 28, 54,
  colour plates 17, 22
brown paper, 34
brown sauce, **11**, 66
brushes, 37, 59-60, 66, 73, 76,
  colour plate 24
BTA, *see* benzotrizaole
bubble wrap, **4**, 31-2, 45-6, 90
buckets, 16
Buckland, 52, **colour plates
  19-21**
buckles, 18, 28, 39, 52, 54,
  colour plates 19-21
bulk finds, 27
burial, burial environment, 7, 22,
  54, 77

Cadw, 83
'Calgon', 65
calico, 80, **colour plate 31**
cames, 18, 42
cancer, 72
carbon, 19
carburization, 19
carcinogen, 72-3
card, cardboard, 34, 44
cast iron, 12
casting, 12-17
  casting bandage, 30
  casting flaws, 53
catheter tubing, **colour plate 32**
cellulose nitrate adhesives, *see*
  adhesives
ceramic, 7, 10, 14, 18
cess-pits, 54
charcoal, 18
Charles II, 29
chasing, 15
chemical cleaning, 8, 59, 62-3, 65
chemicals, 8-10, 36, 55, 62, 64
chipboard, 81
cist cemetery, 17
cisterns, 17
citric acid, *see* acids
cling film, 30
coatings, 54, 71-3, **colour plate 30**
cobalt chloride, 46
cocktail sticks, 60
Code of Practice, 84
Codes of Conduct, 82
coffins, 17
coinage/coins, 14-16, 22, 28-30,
  38-9, 66, 84-5
  radiate coins, 15
cola, **11**, 28, 66
cold working, 12-14, 19
common land, 83
composite objects, 26, 41-2, 46
compressed air tools, 60-1
Conservation Register, 11
consolidants, 73, 76
context, 27-30, 83
Control of Substances Hazardous
  to Health, 63
cooking pots, 16
copper, 12-16, 18, 20-2, 38, 40, 49

copper alloy, 16-18, 23, 40, 47, 52, 54-5, 61, **colour plates 18, 20, 26-7**
copper carbonate, 22-4, **colour plate 2**
copper chloride, 21, 23-4
copper oxide, 23-4, **colour plate 2**
copper sulphides, 23
coroner, 84
corrosion inhibitor, 71
corrosion promoters, 58
COSHH, *see* Control of Substances
cotton, 80
  cotton wool, 44
  cotton wool swabs, 62-3, **colour plate 27**
council bye laws, 83
cracking, 41
cremation urn, 30
crust, 22, 60
'crystal' boxes, **10**, 31-2, 38, 44-5, **colour plates 12, 21**
crystalline structure, 12
cupellation, 17
cuprite, **colour plate 2**
Customs and Excise, 62

decoration, 15, 17, 21, 54, 56, 58
deionised water, 61-2
denture cleaning liquids, 68, **colour plates 28-9**
Department for Culture, Media and Sport, 84
depletion gilding, 14
derelict, 39
desiccated, 68
'Dettol', 68
dies, 15
disinfectants, 68, **colour plate 28**
display, 10, 43, 78-80, **colour plate 31**
  display boards, 79-81
  display cases, 79-81
  display lights, 81
  display materials, 79
distilled water, 61-3
documentation, 55
drawing pins, 81
dress accessories, 16
ductility, 13
dust, 58, 60, 62, 80
  dust hazard, 46
  dust mask, 48, 64, 72, **colour plate 26**
dyestuffs, 68

ear-rings, 14
eastings, 86
EDTA, *see* ethylenediamene tetra-acetic acid
Egypt, 40
electrochemical activity, 67

electrolysis, *see* electrolytic cleaning
electrolytic cleaning, 69
electronic engraving pens, 61
electrum, 14
Elizabeth I, 28
embossing, 16
enamel, 19, 21, 42, 47, 54, 59
English Heritage, 83, 89
engraving, 15
epoxy resin, 76-7
Essendon, 29, **colour plates 9-11**
ethanol, 62
ethylenediamene tetra-acetic acid, 65
eye protection, 64
'eye's only' finds, 27

fan heater, **9**, 41
Federation of Independent Detectorists, 83
felt, 44, 81
  felt-tip pens, 45
FID, *see* Federation of Independent Detectorists
field walking, 7, 27, 31
filigree, 14
Finding our Past, *see* Portable Antiquities Scheme
finds liaison officers, 8, 29, 40, 44, 65, 84-5, 87, 89
findspots, 32, 86
fine metal, *see* pewter
finger rings, 37, 39, **colour plate 1**
firedogs, 18
flavourings, 68
flint, 27-8
flotsam, 39
foam padding, 31-2, **colour plate 12**
'fool's gold', *see* iron pyrites
foreshore, 83
forgery, 76
forging, 12, 19
formaldehydes, 81
formic acid, *see* acids
Fourier Transform, Infrared Spectroscopy, 53
freezer, 42
  freezer storage boxes, 45
fridge, 42
FT-IR, *see* Fourier Transform
fume cupboard, 77
furnace, 17, 19

galena, 17
galvanic corrosion, **colour plate 32**
gap fills, 76-7
garnets, **colour plate 22**
gemstones, 54
  gemstone polishing machines, *see* barelling machines
gilding, 14-15, 21-2

glass, 42, 54, 80
  glass beads, 76
  glass bristle brushes, 60, 66, **colour plate 25**
Global Positioning Systems, 32-**33**, 86
gloves, 38, 48, 60, 63, **colour plates 24, 26**
gold, 12-14, 17, 20-2, 28, 29, 39-40, 45-7, 49, 60, 62, 66, 84
golden iron sulphides, 25
GPS, *see* Global Positioning Systems
granulation, 14
grease, 38, 48, 72
grid references, **3**
grinding wheels, 61

haberdashers, 80
haematite, 54
hammering, 12, 14-16, 19
hand-held dryer, 62
hard solders, *see* solders
hazardous chemicals/residues/vapours, 56, 70, 72
health and safety, 8, 46, 60-3, 72, 77
  health hazards, 60, 63
heat treatments, 70
HMG, 76-7
hoards, **1**, 29-30, 85, **colour plates 9-11**
horn silver, 22
Hoxne, 29
humidity, 9, 21, 41, 43, 71
hydrochloric acid, *see* acids

impressions, 26
impurities, 12, 14-15, 19, 22, 38
IMS, *see* Industrial Methylated Spirit
inappropriate treatments, 10, 58, 64-70
'Incralac', 72-3
indiscriminate cleaning, 21, 59, 67, 69
Industrial Methylated Spirit, 62, 71, **colour plate 27**
inert, 44
ingots, 16-17
inlay, 15-16, 18-19, 21, 52, 59, **colour plate 20**
inorganic materials, 54
instant glues, 76
Institute of Field Archaeologists, 89
internet, 41
interventive conservation, 9-10, 51, 56-64
investigative cleaning/conservation, 57-9
iron, 12-13, 15-16, 18, 20-21, 25, 40, 46-7, 49, 52, 54, 58, 61, 66, **colour plates 3-4, 6, 14-15, 19-21**
Iron Age, 14-16, 18, 29
iron hydroxides, 25
iron oxide, 25, 54

iron phosphate, 25, 54
iron pyrites, 21, 40
iron sulphide, 21
ironworkers, 18
ivory, 47, 54

jet, 47
jetsam, 34
jewellery, 14–16
'Jiffy' foam, 30–1, 38, 44–6, 90
junk, 28, 30, 32, 35

ketchup, **11**, 66–7
knives, 18, 26, 42

labels, 31–2
laboratory, 30, 70–2
lacquer, 55, 71–3, **colour plate 30**
  polyurethene lacquers, 81
lagan, 40
landmarks, 32
latex, 38
lathe, 15, 18
lay metal, *see* pewter
leaching, 24, 54
lead, 12–18, 20, 24–5, 38, 40,
  47, 49, 53, 60, 62, 69, 80–1,
  colour plate 16
  lead carbonates, 24
  lead oxides, 24
  lead sulphides, 17, 24
leather, 22, 26, 32, 47, 54–5, 59,
  colour plates 7–8
legal obligations, 82
legal requirements, 63, 84
lemon juice, **11**, 66
lilac silver corrosion, 22, 49, 54
linen, 80
liquid cleaning dips, 68
loom-weights, 17

magnets, 40
magnifying glass, **8**, 36, 52, 59
malachite, **colour plate 2**
malleability, 12, 15–16, 77
manual cleaning, 59–60, 62, 66,
  colour plates 22, 24
map references, 86
marine environments, 7, 47
masks, 60
mechanical cleaning, 59–60
medieval pewter, *see* pewter
melting points, 12, 18
Merchant Shipping Act, 40
metallurgists, 19
metal foil, 70
metalwork, 30, 38, 73, 79, 82,
  colour plates 9–11
meteoric iron, 12
microballoons, *see* glass beads
micro-environment, 45
micro-organisms, 68
microscope, 13, 30, 36, 51–2,
  59–60, **colour plate 23**

mineral acids, 63
mineral preserved organics, 26,
  54, 67, **colour plates 5–8**
mineralised objects, 23
minerals, 12, 39, 53
mini-drills, 61
mirrors, 16
modelling clay, 81
moral obligations, 82
mould, 13–15, 17, 26, 42, 55
museums, 7, 11, 29–30, 44, 58,
  77, 79, 84, 87, 89

nails, 18, 81
national bodies, 82–83
  National Council for Metal
    Detecting, 82
  National Grid, 86
  Nautical Archaeology Society, 89
  NCMD, *see* National Council
    for Metal Detecting
neatsfoot oil, 74
net-sinkers, 17
newspaper, 34, 44
niello, 15, 19, 21–22
nitrile gloves, 38, 77
noble, 20
non-destructive techniques, 51
northings, 86
nylon thread, 81

oak, 44, 81
object supports, 79
olive oil, 41, 74
orange liquid, 49, **colour plate 14**
Ordnance Survey, 32, 86
ores, 12, 15, 17–18, 20
organic acids, see acids
organics, organic remains/
  residues, 7, 22, 29–30, 42, 47,
  53–5, 58, 65, 72, 74
original surface, 19–26, 39, 52,
  58–60, 62–3, **colour plates
  21, 26**
oven, 48–9
oxygen, 20, 39, 41, 46, 66,
  colour plate 4

packing, packing materials, 8,
  32, 36, 41, 43–5, 48, 89–90
paper, 44
'Paraloid B72', 73, 76, 90
parks, 83
partial vacuum, 71
pastiches, 76
pastureland, **5**, 83
patinas, 15, 17, 21–2, 24
patterns, 17
pendants, 53
permanent pens, 31–32, 45, 90
personal liability insurance, 82
perspex, 80
  perspex brackets, 80
  perspex mounts, 90
  perspex pegs, 80

petroleum jelly ('Vaseline'), 41,
  68, 73
pewter, 18, 24–5, 47
  Britannia metal, 18
  fine metal, 18
  lay metal, 18
  medieval pewter, 18
  Roman pewter, 18
phosphates, 54
phosphoric acid, *see* acids
phosphorus, 19
photographs, 55–6
pigs (lead), 17
pilgrim badges, 53
pins, 18, 28, 54, 80, **colour
  plates 31–2**
pipes (lead), 17
piridine, 62
planishing, 15
'Plastazote', 36, 44–5, 80, 90,
  colour plates 12–13, 31
plaster, 47
  plaster of Paris, 30
plastic covered pins, 80, **colour
  plate 31**
plastic padding, 77
plating, 16–17, 19, 52, 58
ploughland, 27, 83
ploughs, 18, 77
ploughsoil, **1**, 28
plugs (lead), 18
pneumatic pen, 37, 60–1, **colour
  plate 26**
polishing wheels, 61
pollutants, 9, 21, 58, 71, 81
polyester, 80
  polyester paste, 77
  polyester resins, 77
polyether foam, 45–6
polypropelene boxes, 45
polystyrene boxes, 31, 44–5, 90,
  colour plate 31
polythene, 30
  polythene bags, **2**, **4**, **10**, 31–2,
    44, 46, 48, 90
  polythene boxes, 31, **38**, 45,
    89–90
  polythene foam, 44–5
  polythene labels, 31, 45, 90
polyurethene foam, **colour
  plate 10**
polyurethene lacquers, *see*
  lacquers
popular cleaning methods, 57,
  65–70
Portable Antiquities Scheme, 7–
  8, 82, 85, 87
pottery, 9, 27, 30, 42
powder pigments, 77
powered tools, 60
preventive conservation, 9–10,
  43, 58
provenance, 58
puffer, **colour plate 24**
punches, 15–16
PVC plastic, 81

quenching, 19, 70
quick fix treatments, 65

radiate coins, *see* coins
radiators, 41, 81
raised, raising, 15
razors, 18
Receiver of Wreck, 30, 85
reconstruction, 74-6
Regional Museum Councils, 89
relative humidity, 46-7
relative humidity indicating
  strips, **10**, 45, 48, 90, **colour
  plate 12**
'Renaissance Wax', 73, **colour
  plate 30**
repair, 9, 74-6
reporting obligations, 64
repoussé, 16
reshaping, 40, 75, 77, 84
restoration, 9, 74-7
reversibility, 75
reversible treatments, 10, 57, 72, 76
RH, *see* relative humidity
rivets, rivetting, 13, 15-16
rolling, 12
Roman, **1**, 12, 15-16, 19, 54,
  colour plates 17, 27
  Roman pewter, *see* pewter
rotary tools, 61, 63
rotivators, 77
rubber based foams, 44
rust, 20

salt, **11**, 15, 38, 54, 61, 65, 67,
  72, **colour plate 28**
scabbards, 18-19, 26, 54
scales, 41, 49
scalpels, 59-60, **colour plate 24**
Scanning Electron Microscopy, 53
Scheduled Ancient Monuments, 83
scrapers, 59
sealant, 80
seals, 53
seam lines, 53
self-indicating silica gel, *see* silica gel
self-seal polyethylene bags, 31, 44
SEM, *see* Scanning
shale, 47
sheaths, 19
sheet lead, 14, 16, 58
shield, 16, **colour plates 7-8**
shield boss, **colour plate 23**
SHMP, *see* 'Calgon'
signs of trouble, 36, 49, 71,
  colour plates 14-18
silica gel, **10**, 45-9, 81, 90,
  colour plate 12
  self-indicating, 46, 48-9
silk, 81
silver, 12-14, 16-17, 20-2, 28-9,
  38-40, 45, 47, 49, 60, 62, 66,
  77, 84, **colour plates 20, 25**

silver chloride, 22, 49
silver cleaning cloth, 70
silver dips, 68
silver gilt, **colour plate 22**
silver sulphide, 15, 22
'Silvo', 68
slag, 17, 19
small finds, 28
smelt, smelting, 12-13, 16-18
Snettisham, 14, **colour plates 1, 5**
soap, 68
socketed axes, 17-18
sodium chloride, 61, 67
sodium hydroxide, 69
sodium sequicarbonate, 65
soft solders, *see* solders
solders, 13-16, 18, 54
  hard solders, 14
  soft solders, 14
solvents, 61-4, 68, 73, 77,
  colour plate 22
spears, spearheads, 18, 26,
  colour plate 11
speculum, 16, 40
spoons, 15, 39
SSC, *see* sodium sequicarbonate
stabilisation treatments, 70-1
staples, 81
steel, 19
'Steradent', 68
'Stewart' boxes, 31
sticky tape, 60
stone, 7, 10, 14, 47, 54
storage, storage materials, 8, 36,
  39, 42-9, 56, 71, 80, 89-90
striking, 15
sulphuric acid, *see* acids
sump oil, 74
sunlight, 41, 81
surface enrichment, 17
Sutton Hoo, 75
swords, 18, 26, **colour plates 4, 11**
synthetic polymers, 73

table salt, *see* salt
tableware, 15, 18
tap water, **7**, 36, 61, 65
tarnish, 20, 22, 38, 68-70, 81
textile, 22, 26, 47, 59, 80-1,
  colour plates 5-6
thermohygrometer, **colour
  plate 12**
tidal water, 40, 85
tin, 12-14, 16-18, 20, 24, 40, 49, 53
  tin foil, 70
  tin oxide, 24
tissue paper, 34, 44, 60
tobacco, 64
tomato ketchup, *see* ketchup
tools, 9, 16, 18-19, 36, 59-61,
  63-64, 78, **colour plate 24**
torcs, 14

toxic, 8, 26, 38, 55, **colour
  plate 5**
trace elements, 12
treasure, 29, 36, 39-40, 82-3
  Treasure Act, 8, 28, 39, 84-5,
  colour plate 1
  Treasure Trove, 82, 84
tungsten lights, 81
'Tupperware' boxes, **4**, 31-2, 44
tweezers, **colour plate 24**
'Tyvek' labels, 31, 45, 90 *see* also
  polythene labels

UKIC, see United Institute
ultrasonic cleaning tanks, 70
United Kingdom Institute for
  Conservation, 11, 88

'Vaseline', see petroleum jelly
'Velcro', **colour plate 31**
vessels, 15-16, 18, 30, 58
vinegar, **11**, 66
visual inspection, 51, **colour
  plate 23**
vivianite, 54

wadding, 68
warts (corrosion), 24
water based glues, 81
waterlogged
  environments/conditions, 21,
  23-5, 32, 35, 42, 46-7, 54-5,
  colour plate 4
waxes, 68, 73, **colour plate 30**
'WD-40', 41, 74
weapons, 16, 18, 78
'weeping', **colour plate 14**
weights, 17
welding, 14
wet cleaning, 61-2
Wetwang, **colour plate 3**
'white finger', 61
white gold, 14
white heat, 14
window grilles, 18
wire, 12, 14
wire brushes, 66
wood, 10, 14, 18, 22, 26, 30, 44,
  47, 54-5, 59, 80-1, **colour
  plates 7-8**
  wood composites, 81
wool, 44, 81
wreck, 21, 39-40, 64, 82, 85
wrought iron, 12, 19

x-radiography, 51-3, 55-6, 58-9,
  colour plates 20-1, 23

zinc, 16, 54